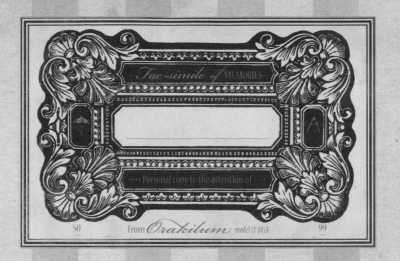

Fac-simile of MEMORIES

Personal copy to the attention of

50   from Orakilum model 12-245A   99

[ORAKILUM : 1ST SERIES]
MODEL 12-24.5A

Index of files
The Park of Chimeras – London

YEAR	File No.	Report No.	Place / Location	Time Period	No. of Creatures	~ Observations ~
1850	0001	0001	Kensington Gardens + Hyde Park	Summer	20	....CREATION OF LONDON PARK OF THE CHIMERAS....
		0002	St James Park	Autumn	33	Domain of the Wild opened
		0003	Regent's Park	Winter	33	....ROSE GARDEN OPENED....
		0004	Kew Gardens	Spring	37	....LARGE GREENHOUSE OPENED....
1851	0002	0005-0008	×	×	37	....N.T.R....
1852	0003	0009-0012	THE 5 PARKS	×××	37	....NORTHERN ALLEYS ENLARGED....
1853	0004	0013-0016	×	×	41	....ADMISSION OF 4 BLACK HYDRAS....
1854	0005	0017-0020	Kensington Gardens	Winter +	42	Arrival of a Dragon (very young)
1855	0006	0021-0024	×	×	42	× [n.t.r.]
1856	0007	0025-0028	Kew Gardens	Winter ++	45	....ARRIVAL OF 3 UNDINES....
1857	0008	0029-0032	St. James Park	×	45	....N.T.R....
1858	0009	0033-0036	×	Summer +	45	....INSPECTION OF FOUNTAIN WATER....
1859	0010	0037-0038	Regent's Park	Autumn	46	....ADMISSION OF THE PHANTOM (125) OF THE DOCKS - NORTHERN AREA....
		0039-0040	Regent's Park	Winter	47	....ADMISSION OF THE PHANTOM OF THE DOCKS - SOUTHERN AREA....
1860 to 1865	0011	0041-0064	Hyde Park	×	47	....ARRIVAL OF FILIBERT BOHRUZIG....
						security optimised as far as I'm concerned
1866	0012	0065	Kew Gardens	×	47	....GREENHOUSE REPAIRS & MAINTENANCE (WINDOWS + 25)....
		0066-0068	××××			
1867	0013	0069-0072	St. James Park	Spring	52	....ADMISSION OF 5 GHOSTS....
1868	0014	0073-0076	×	Winter	52	....NORTH AND WEST GATES REFURBISHED....
1869	0015	0077-0080	××××	××××	52	×
1870	0016	------		------	52	....TECHNICAL PROBLEM (MAINTENANCE)....
1871	0017	0085-0088	××××	××××	52	South Gate repaired ....N.T.R. ~~[illegible]~~....
1872/1873	0018/19	0089-0096	Kew Gardens	August 7th	53	....ADMISSION OF S. MOR....
			××××	Winter ++	54	....ADMISSION OF J. DELALUNE....
1874	0021	0101-0102	Regent's Park	Autumn	56	....INCIDENT OF OCT. 10TH/EXPLOSION - BREACH IN PARK.. North Gate
		0103-0104	THE 5 PARKS	Winter	56	....FOG....
1875	0020	0097-0100	Hyde Park	Summer & Winter	56	....ADMISSION OF 2 GRIFFINS (COUPLE).... Ghost hunt!!

1B

111011 111

×××××× ××××

×× ××××××

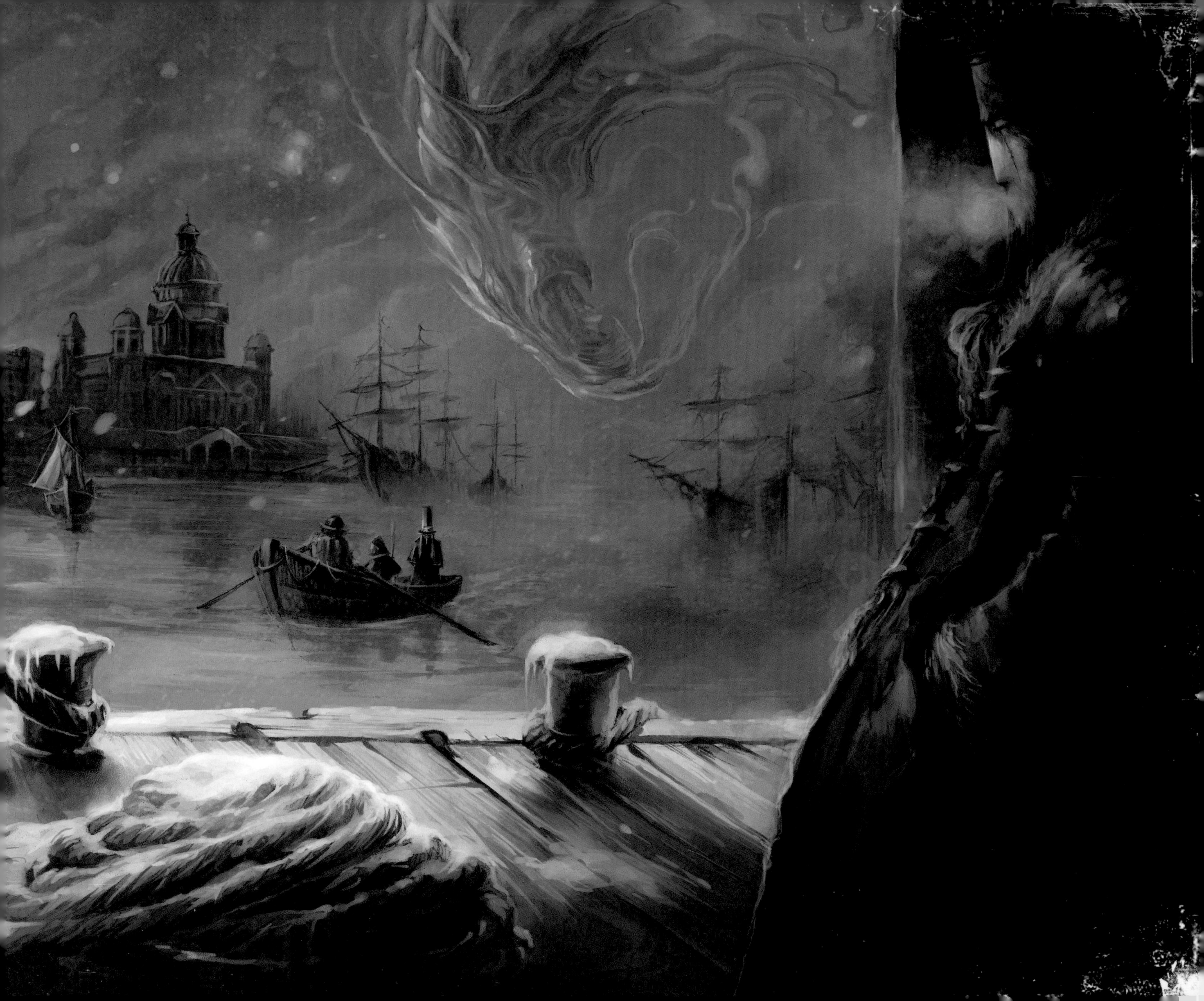

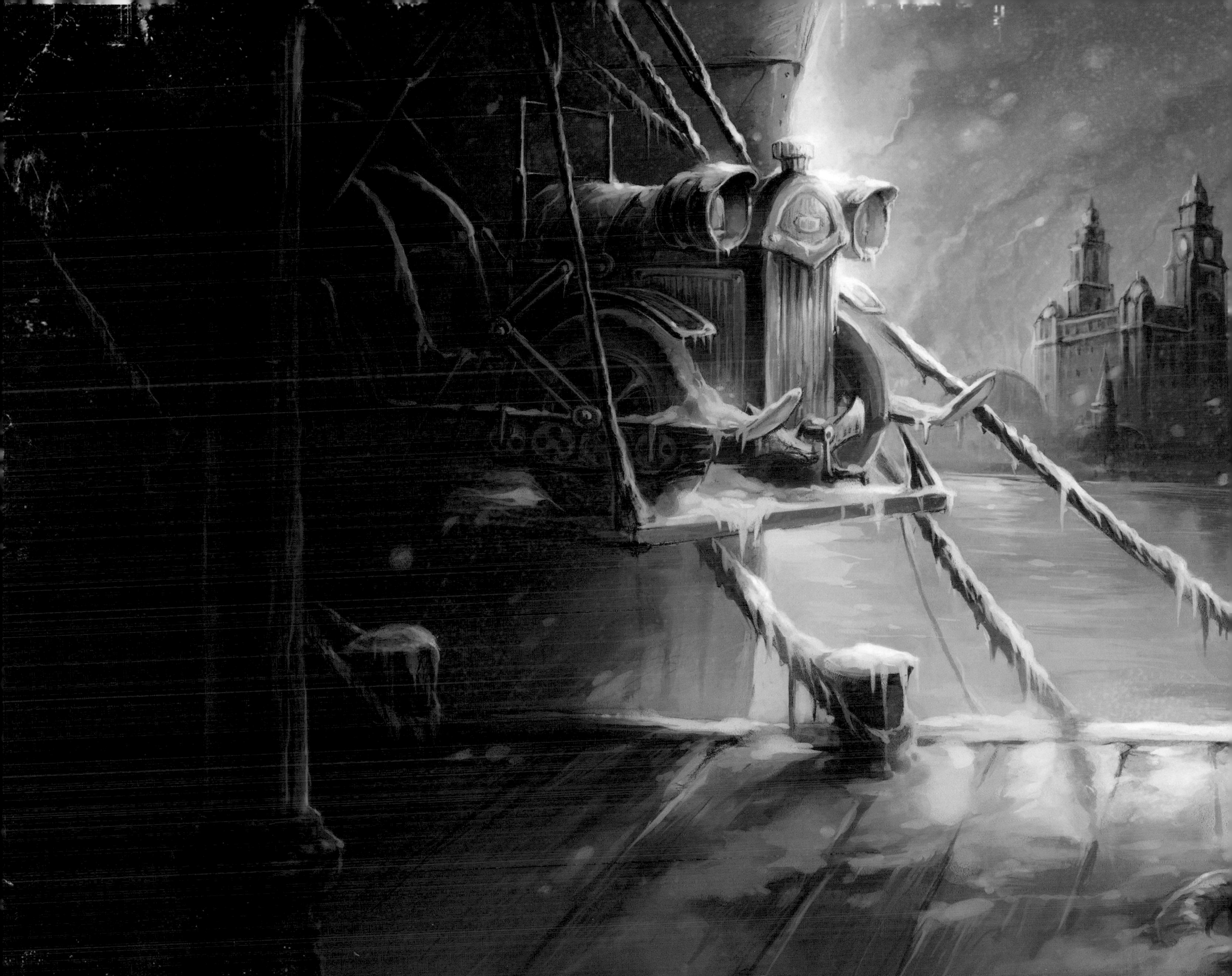

THE CHASE HAS ONLY JUST BEGUN —*Liverpool, Dec. 31, 1899, 5:00 a.m. GMT* - CITY ARCHIVE IMAGE VIA *Orakilum*

Location .... LONDON

Sender .... SIR THÉODORE JOLICŒUR POPPINS

OFFICIAL WARDEN OF THE GARDEN OF SHADOWS

To .... ORDER OF ARCHITECTS

++++++ ++++++ ++++++ ++++++ TRANSFER SUCCESSFUL/COMPLETE

—PARK OF THE CHIMERAS ++++

FINAL CLOSING ++++++

after 11.00 a.m.

CALL. 0044++

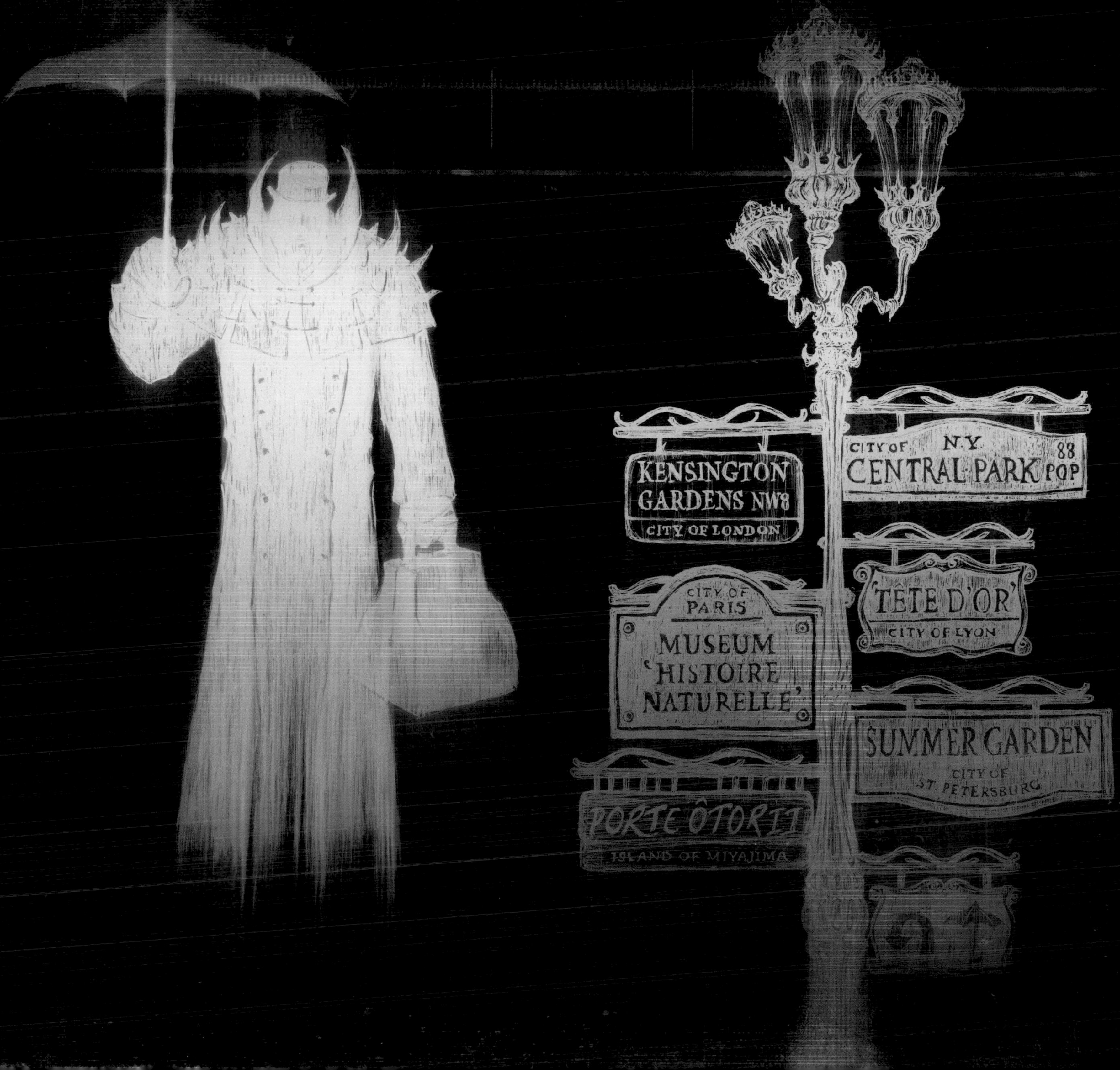
KENSINGTON GARDENS NW8
CITY OF LONDON
CITY OF N.Y.
CENTRAL PARK
88 POP
CITY OF PARIS
MUSEUM 'HISTOIRE NATURELLE'
TÊTE D'OR
CITY OF LYON
SUMMER GARDEN
CITY OF ST. PETERSBURG
PORTE ÔTORII
ISLAND OF MIYAJIMA

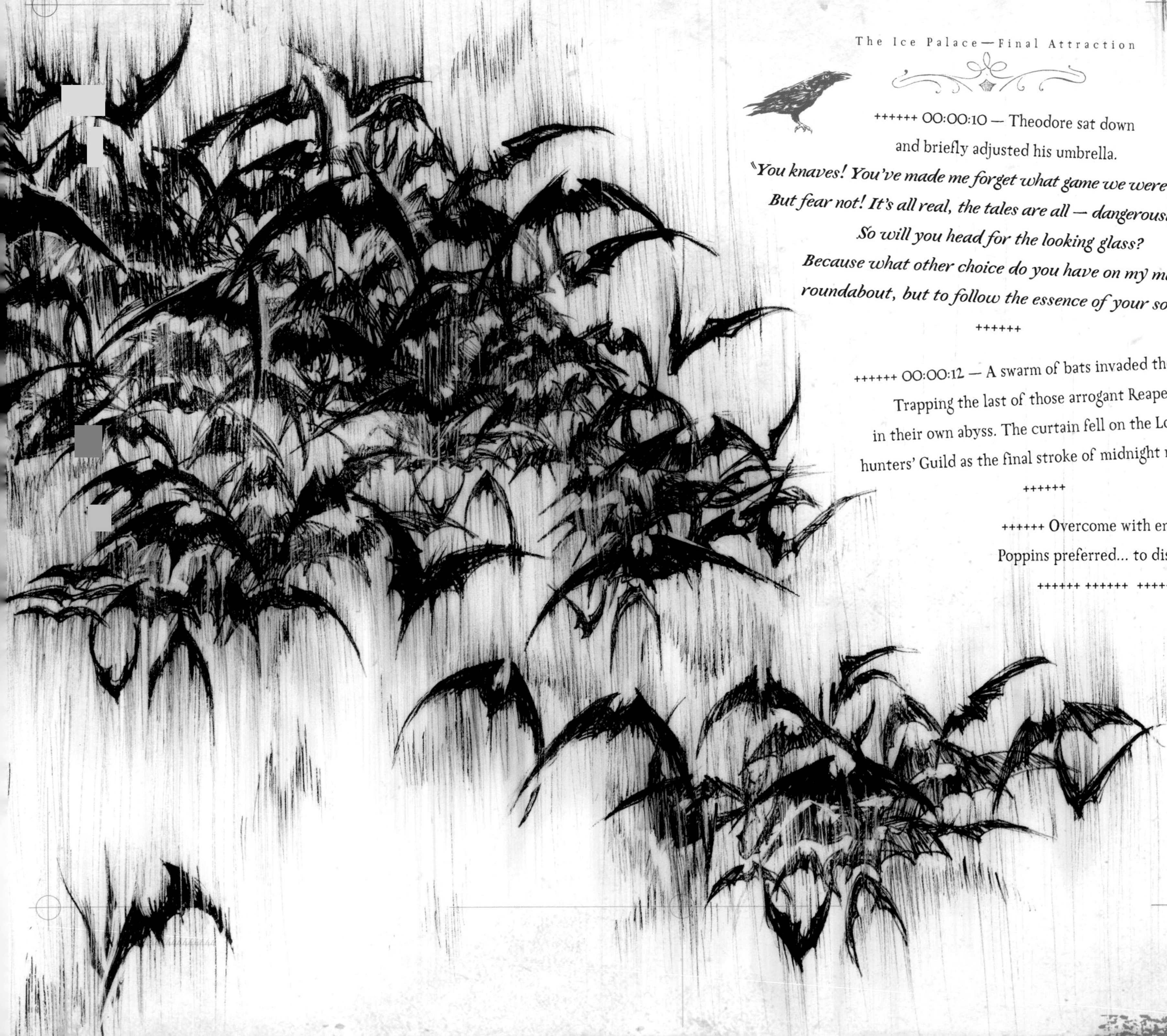

The Ice Palace—Final Attraction

++++++ 00:00:10 — Theodore sat down
and briefly adjusted his umbrella.

*"You knaves! You've made me forget what game we were playing here!
But fear not! It's all real, the tales are all — dangerously — true.
So will you head for the looking glass?
Because what other choice do you have on my magic
roundabout, but to follow the essence of your soul?"*

++++++

++++++ 00:00:12 — A swarm of bats invaded the scene.
Trapping the last of those arrogant Reapers
in their own abyss. The curtain fell on the London
hunters' Guild as the final stroke of midnight rang out.

++++++

++++++ Overcome with emotion,
Poppins preferred... to disappear.

++++++ ++++++ ++++++

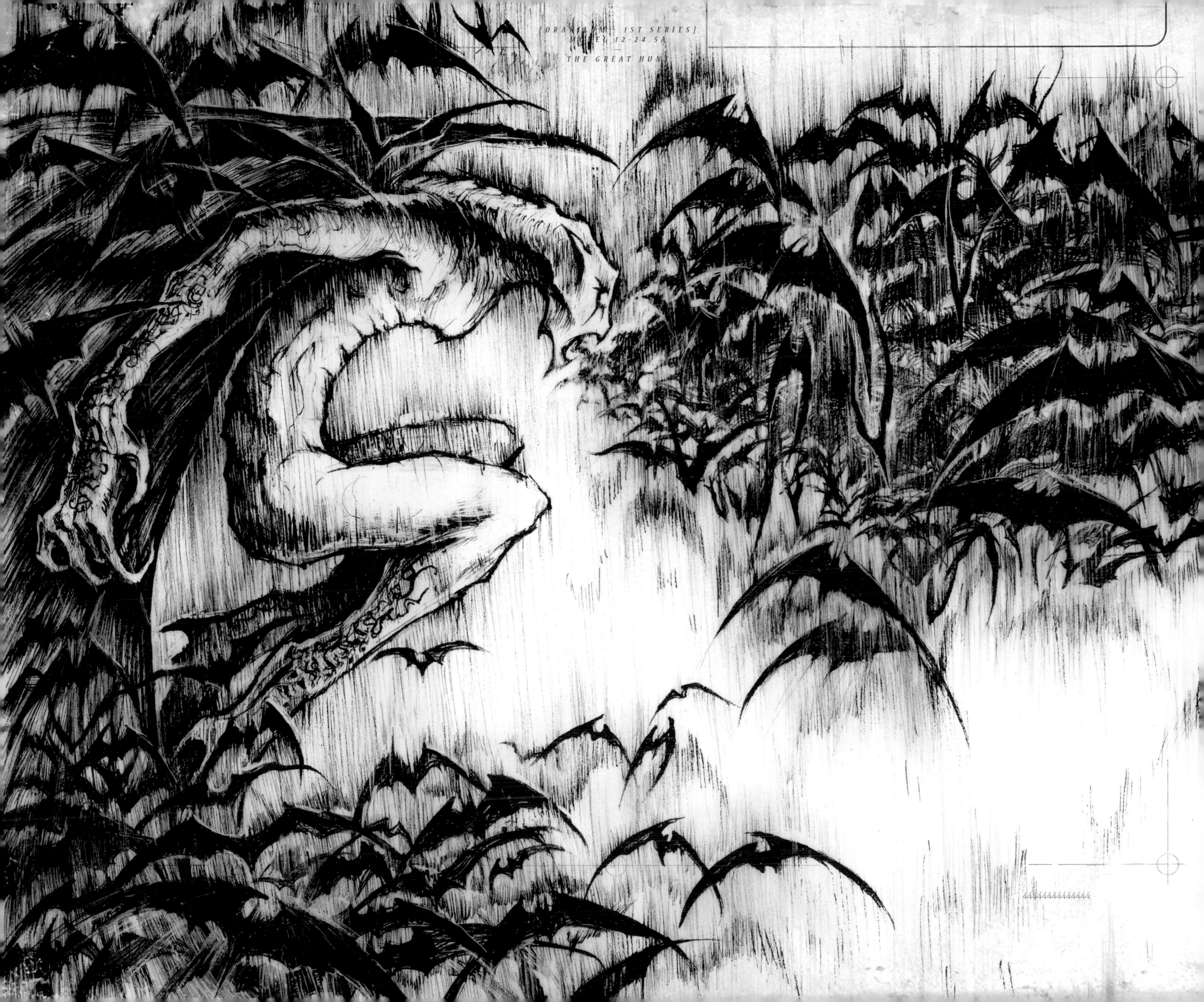
1ST SERIES]
12-24.5A
THE GREAT HUNT

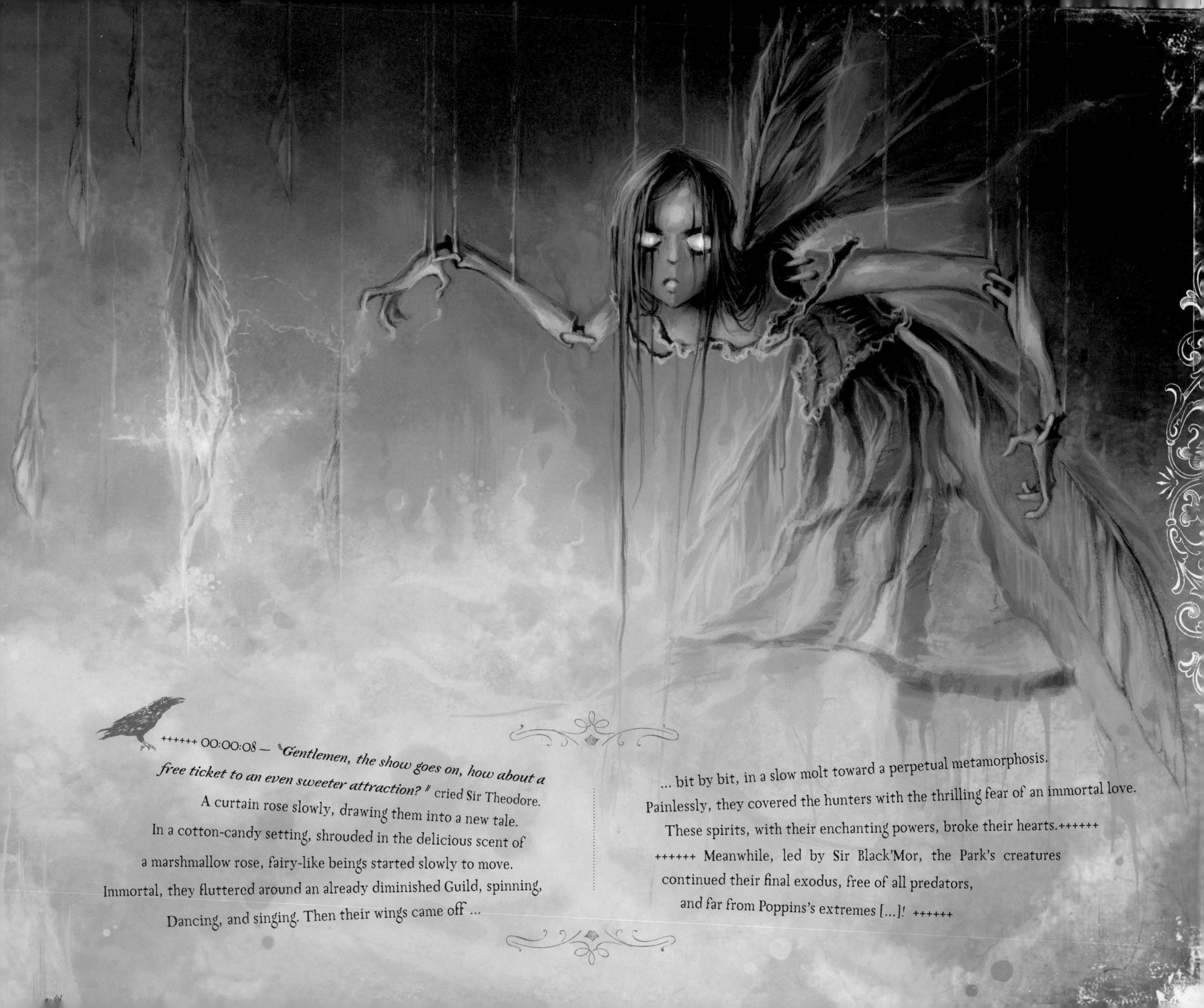

++++++ 00:00:08 — *"Gentlemen, the show goes on, how about a free ticket to an even sweeter attraction?"* cried Sir Theodore.

A curtain rose slowly, drawing them into a new tale.

In a cotton-candy setting, shrouded in the delicious scent of

a marshmallow rose, fairy-like beings started slowly to move.

Immortal, they fluttered around an already diminished Guild, spinning,

Dancing, and singing. Then their wings came off ...

... bit by bit, in a slow molt toward a perpetual metamorphosis.

Painlessly, they covered the hunters with the thrilling fear of an immortal love.

These spirits, with their enchanting powers, broke their hearts.++++++

++++++ Meanwhile, led by Sir Black'Mor, the Park's creatures

continued their final exodus, free of all predators,

and far from Poppins's extremes [...]! ++++++

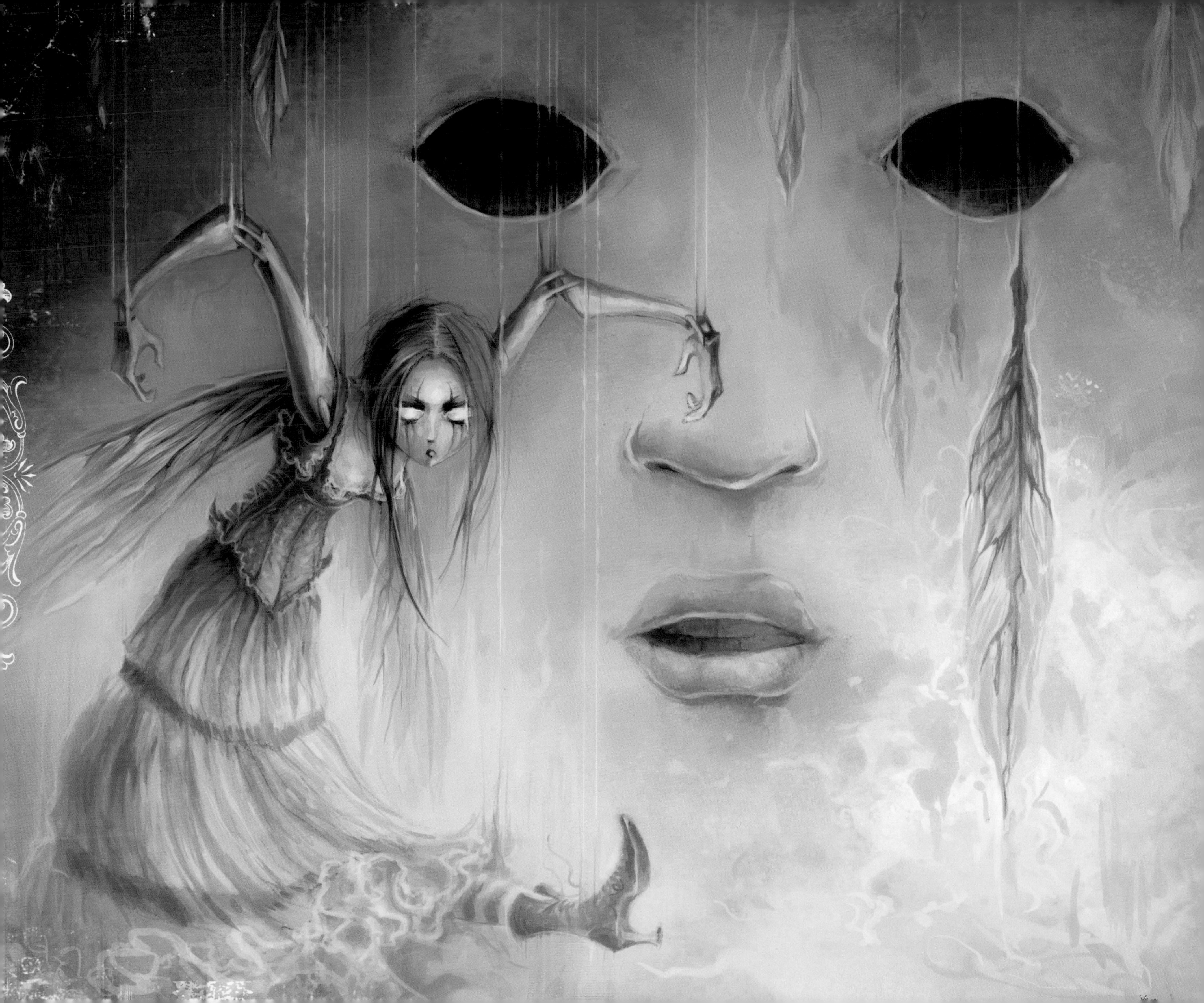

THEODORE POPPINS PRESENTS
Play again with Ghost Duelists!
DUEL OF GHOSTS
Icon of the HORROR COLLECTION
In the heart of KENSINGTON GARDENS
1859
18-08-11

Report CLXXXVII ~ B-I

4th strike

THE PHANTOM DUELISTS

++++++ ***Polysynchronic connection to subjects Theodore Jolicœur Poppins and Sir Elian Black'Mor for remote retrieval of memories*** : ++++++ ++++++ ++++++ ++++++
— 00:00:04 — Two severely injured Centaurs arrive
— 00:00:05 — Blinded by ***Møãt-Tarvaa's*** hypnotic orbs in the hazy skies of the capital, they come running, feverish, from the four corners of London. As expected, dazzled by its own greed, the Guild is at the gates of Regent's Park. A hunter mocks Sir Theodore:
“***The Hare is finally flushed out!***”
Poppins smiles.
++++++ ++++++ +++++
++++++ ++++++
++++++

++++++ 00:00:07 — It's too late to turn back! They are carried away by the vision of a monstrous mouth of twisted roots. Becalmed, Theodore nodded: “***Well done, gentleman Dream Robbers, you just entered the breach!***” ++++++ ++++++ ++++++
++++++ ++++++ ++++++ ++++++
++++++ ++++++ ++++++
++++++ ++++++
++++++ ++++++ ++++++
++++++ ++++++ ++++++ ++++++ ++++++

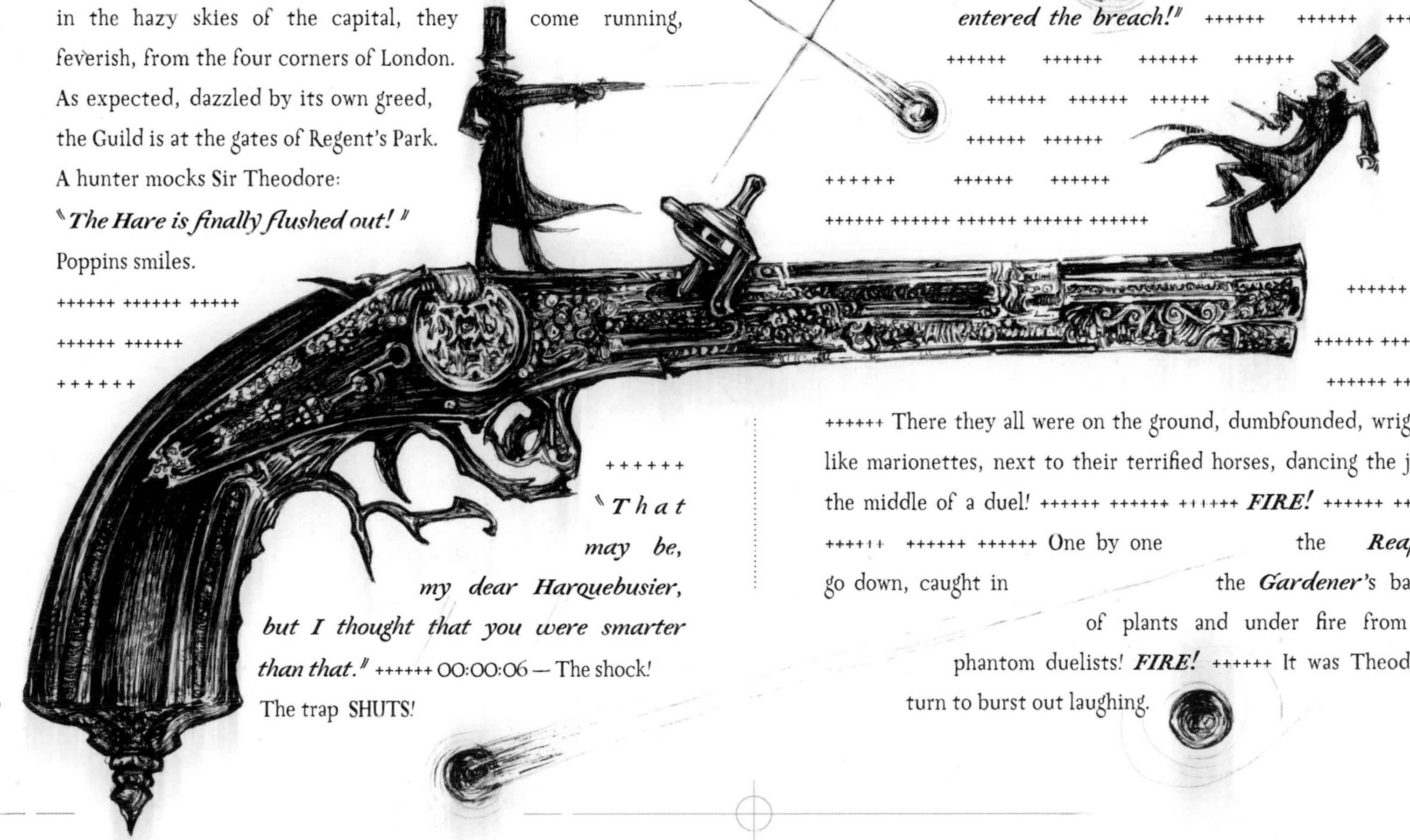

++++++ VERY DROLL!
++++++ ++++++ ++++++
++++++ ++++++ ++++++
++++++ ++++++

++++++
“***That may be, my dear Harquebusier, but I thought that you were smarter than that.***” ++++++ 00:00:06 — The shock! The trap SHUTS!

++++++ There they all were on the ground, dumbfounded, wriggling like marionettes, next to their terrified horses, dancing the jig in the middle of a duel! ++++++ ++++++ ++++++ ***FIRE!*** ++++++ ++++++ ++++++ ++++++ ++++++ One by one the ***Reapers*** go down, caught in the ***Gardener***'s barrier of plants and under fire from the phantom duelists! ***FIRE!*** ++++++ It was Theodore's turn to burst out laughing.

THE BULLETS FLY IN THIS PAPER MACHE *MASQUERADE*

—Regent's Park, Dec. 27, 1899, 00:00 a.m. GMT

EXTRACTED MEMORY OF *T. Poppins* RETRANSCRIBED BY *Orakilum*

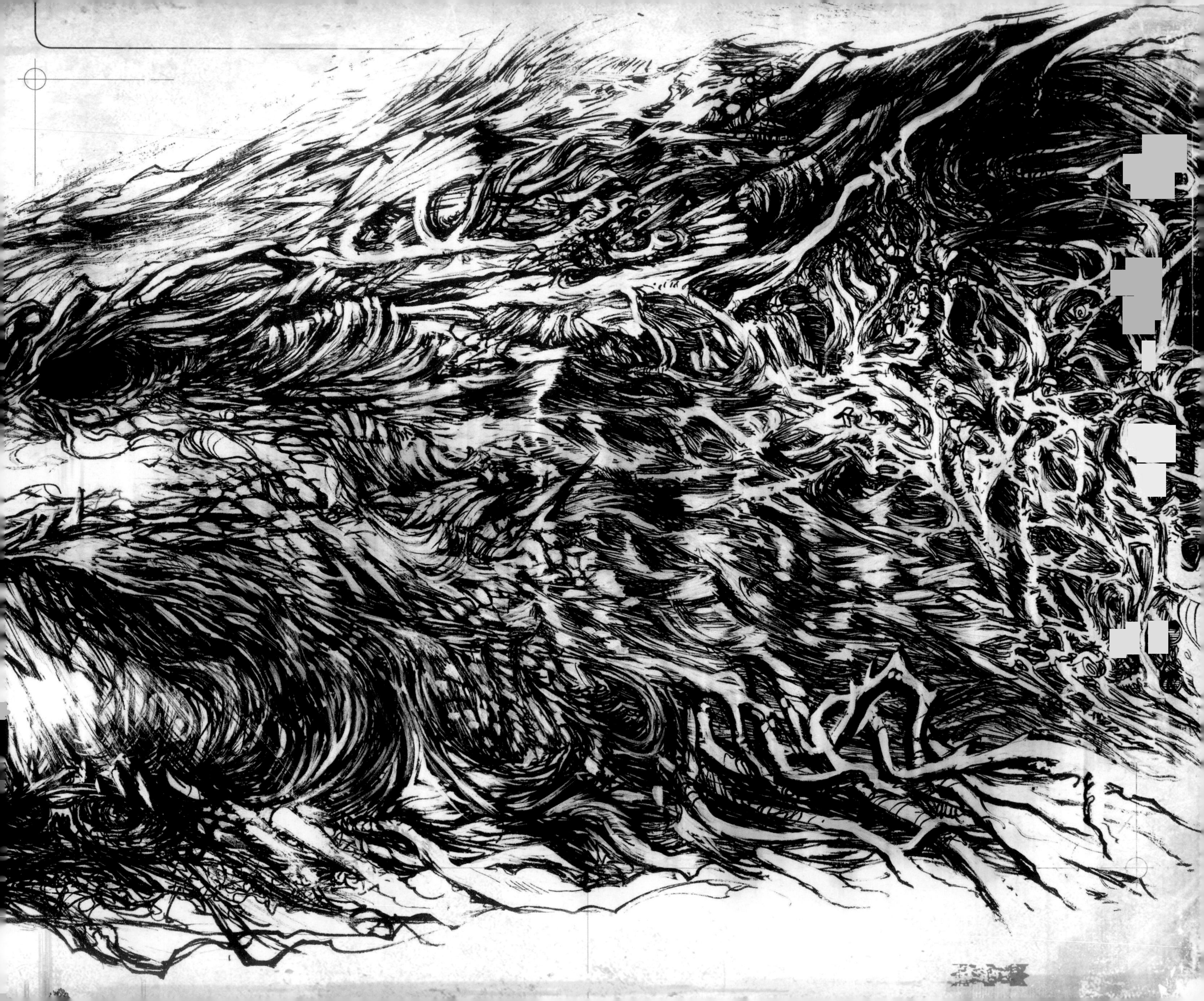

Report CLXXXVII ∼ B-I

2nd strike

IN THE JAWS OF THE WOLF

Second strike of midnight ++++++ ++++++ ++++++ ++++++ ++++++ **STEAM POWER AND PAPER MACHE!!** ++++++ *Welcome to my fantastic funfair.* ++++++ ++++++ ++++++ Do you see that pale shadow, that gaping mouth, which swallows souls? I am preparing it for them, the ones who wanted to hunt the Dragon, skin the Titans, possess the Golem's heart, all the while ruining and exploiting the good nature of Fairies. That's enough! I'm ready for all these little princes, petty bourgeois, faux gentlemen with tawdry memories who have caused this madness! Let them be happy! I accept the challenge! It's been decided, I'll accompany them into the middle of this macabre dance, except that this time, I'll be the one who's dealing the cards and playing the game, which I already know I've won! Turnabout is fair play. I'll be taking those Dream Reapers for a ride in my phantom dream train. And I will be its sole driver. When those hunters cross the breach, they will get lost in the jungle of its roots. Engrossed by their fears they will be engulfed in a nightmare, my nightmare. ++++++ It'll take place during the chaos of the funfair. Sir Elian will do it, he's the only one who can open the London portal, the gateway that leads to the lost passageways, the paths to the Land Beyond Dreams.

++++++ I, Theodore Jolicœur Poppins ++++++ ++++++

++++++ Warden of the Park the of Chimeras ++++++

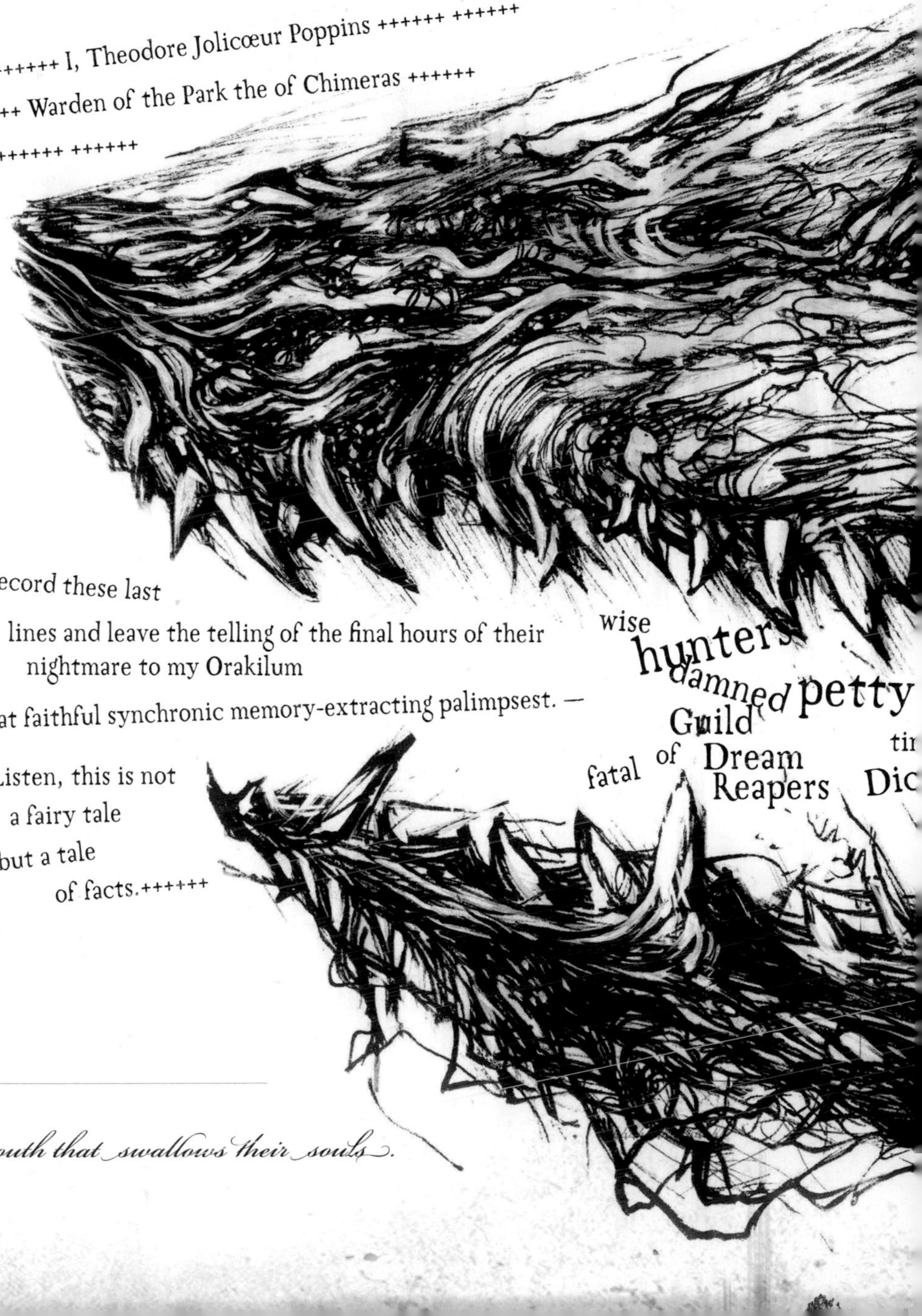

++++++ ++++++

record these last

lines and leave the telling of the final hours of their nightmare to my Orakilum

— that faithful synchronic memory-extracting palimpsest. —

Listen, this is not a fairy tale but a tale of facts. ++++++

wise hunters damned petty Guild fatal of Dream tir Reapers Dic

For them, the breach will become a gaping mouth that swallows their souls.

2ª

Theodore's NIGHTMARE

Report CLXXXVII ∼ B-I

46ᵀᴴ file

FROM THE YEAR 1899

THE ART OF HUNTING

13 UMBRELLA 'POPS' INTO A
NIGHTMARE

THE OUTCOME OF THE
BATTLE IS INEVITABLE
T. POPPINS

++++++ Could taking on this jumble of files be my punishment? A purgatory that I inflict upon myself as a bureaucratic respite? *burden!* [...]

++++++ I was moved by the portraits of these **cursed creatures** attached to these meager reports — piles of copies, hundreds of memory extracts — sent to the designers over forty-nine years. More than two hundred have found sanctuary in the shelter of my Park.

++++++ But how many still wander, hunted? (I'm digressing and it's making my head spin.) Time is running out! The hunters are on the prowl, tracking far too close to my perimeter. They want their new hunt and they shall have it. But those gentlemen will have to wait! [...] I still have to pick up the two injured Centaurs who managed to flee the wilds of Dartmoor. These mythological beings — the last of Pan's children still in England — cannot be left behind. What could they be doing? A week has passed since they were supposed to cross the Kew Gardens Bridge. ++++++ ++++++ ++++++ ++++++

+ + + +

+ + + + +

+ + + + + +

+ + + + + +

+ + + + + +

+ + + + +

For five days and six nights without interruption, there has been rustling in the alleys, whispering in the greenhouse, impatient whining and complaining in the woods.

++++++ *The whisperers are murmuring and driving me mad with their predictions!* We cannot wait much longer. The first stroke of midnight just rang out. The time has come for me to enter the scene. I've always known that humans like to scare themselves, which is lucky because that's what I do best!

++++++ *I'll be their worst nightmare.*

I feel the breach coming to life. It's getting impatient.

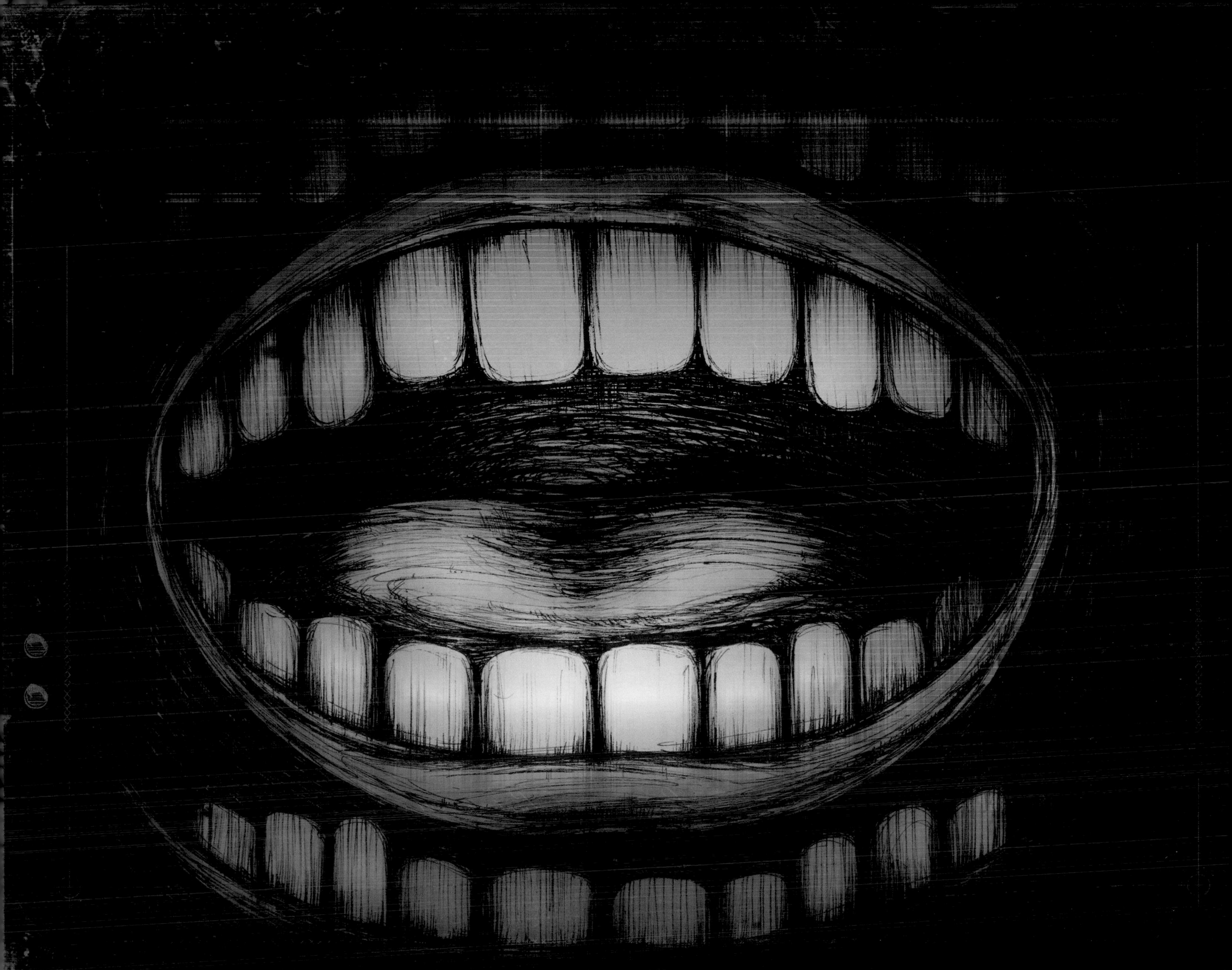

—Regent's Park, the evening of Dec. 26, 1899, 10:42 p.m. GMT - ILLUSTRATED MEMORY VIA *Orakilum*

46TH FILE

[ORAKILUM : 1ST SERIES]
MODEL 12 - 24.5A

THE GREAT HUNT
1899

187th REPORT {Book I} __ *From Regent's Park to St James Park*

8-7-72

THE JUNK, TEMPORARY ABERRATION

2ᴮ

It goes without saying that I have no right to question his role, but still, I can't help wondering.

Kensington Gardens
Serpentine
Dark Water
2
4
b
b

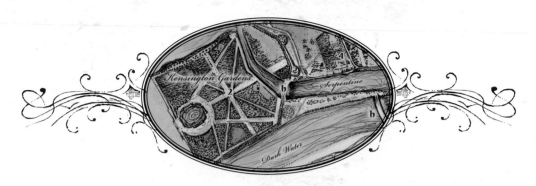

2 Fair Grounds - 4 Little Theatre - b Bridges

++++++ Since his arrival, the lines and curves have gotten longer and larger — like doomed veins in a heart. They seem to poison his soul and instigate his fateful role as the *human key.* ++++++ I am hastening to transmit this report because I know the importance of its revelations on upcoming events. The whisperers already sense their coming. According to them, within a few days, the hunters will be at our doorstep. The echoes of their murmurs heighten the creatures' distress. I don't know why, but for safety's sake, I went to retrieve an old prediction* from my gear. It confirms what they have been mumbling. ++++++ ++++++ ++++++ ++++++ ++++++ ++++++ ++++++ ***We are Cursed!*** ++++++ ++++++ ++++++

* In the In-octavo, the date, time and place are the same.

++++++ ***The battle approaches.*** ++++++ ++++++ ++++++ ++++++ As I just confirmed to you (through backdated memory), Sir Elian Black'Mor is going to do what he came here for.++++++ ++++++ ++++++ ++++++ ++++++ ***It's the only solution!*** ++++++ ++++++ If history repeats itself, as it did once on the plains of Yeun Elez, all sounds in the city will be swallowed up, and London will become silent. Even if doing this reveals our intentions to the Guild, there is no other way! We have to act quickly! The hunters won't be deceived — they'll recognize the traces of the passage — and the open breach. I have no time to tell you any more. ++++++ ***The cock is crowing, I am expected...***

END OF THE REPORT ON THE REMEMBRANCE OF A LONG CROSSING

—HYDE PARK ++++++

THE KEY, DEC. 08, 1899 - 06 A.M. - GMT

PERSONAL

Theodore P.

2

4444444444444

Report CLXXXVI ∼ B-3-c

day **07**

PAN PULLS THE STRINGS

++++++ **MY GOD UMBRELLA!** I can't write any more! *By the magic ribs of my umbrella*, my hands are tired, I shudder, and cannot forget the image of that junk being swallowed in a storm of hydras and foam. I'm haunted by this extracted memory, clearly from his crossing... In fact, I'm afraid, *afraid of Pan's macabre games*. I fear that he has manipulated Sir Elian in order to save his children. Had sadness blinded him to it?

++++++ ++++++ ++++++

++++++ ++++++ ++++++

++++++ ++++++

I cannot accept that he knowingly ordered the massacre of the crew for the sole purpose of getting this ghost ship to the gates of the Land Beyond Dreams.

++++++ No, that's pretty far-fetched, (the Guild's exasperating attacks on the park are getting more and more accurate and turning me into a nervous wreck!) Is it possible, or even conceivable that Pan could have instigated such a massacre on board? *(I fear your answer...)* Into what hybrid had this *Alchemist* transformed him during his crossing of the North Pole during the winter of 1894?

++++++ ++++++ He embarked as a man and came back as a *Dream Smuggler*, bound to the two worlds. ++++++

++++++ ++++++ ++++++ ++++++

Pan's plan was taking shape right in front of my eyes. ++++++ ++++++ ++++++

++++++ I discerned tattoos on his left arm that are more than just mythological designs...

Anyone who speaks with the Alchemist, our worlds' great dreamer, will emerge with an enlightened soul.

Is Pan just having fun pulling our strings?

44444444444444

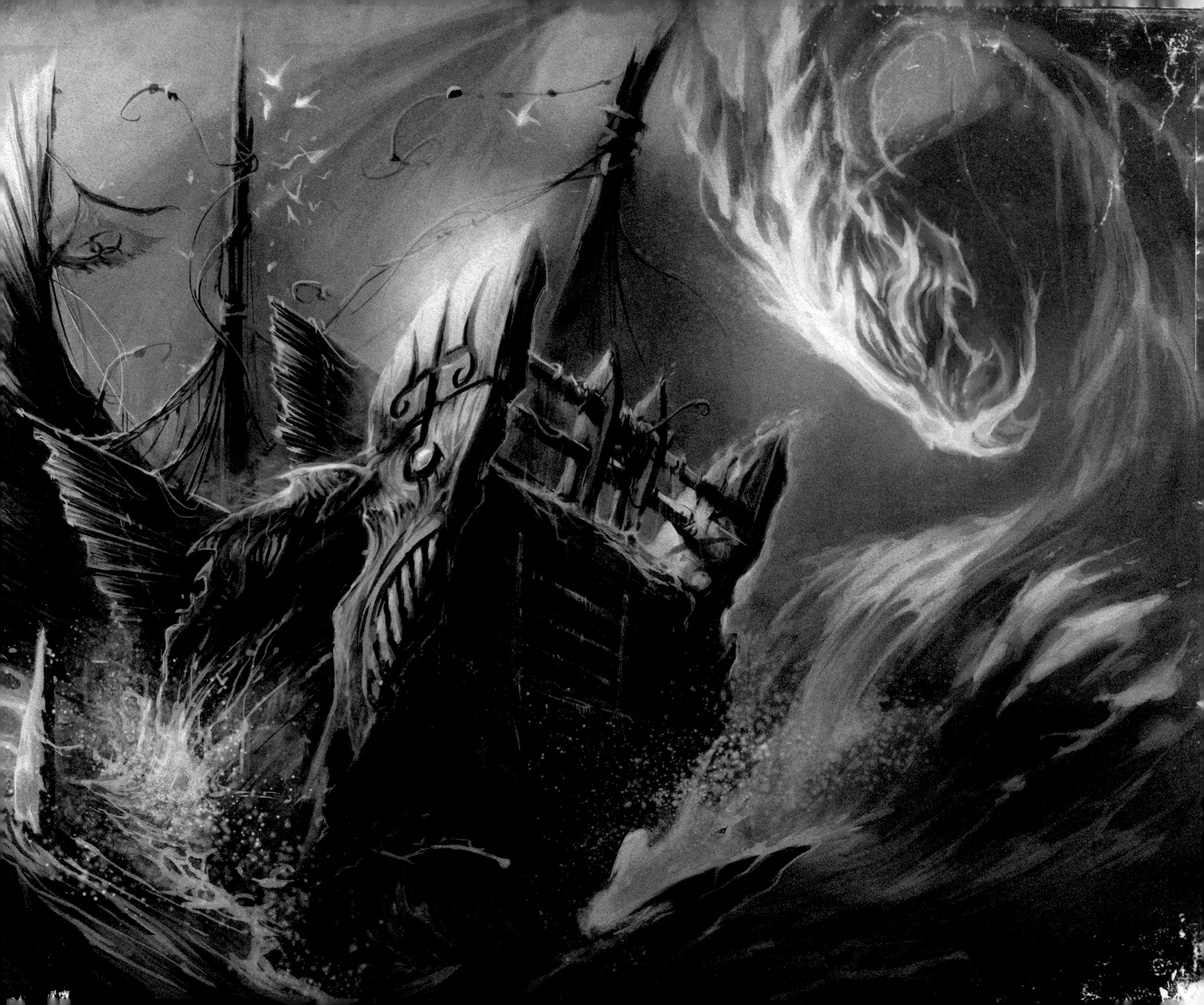

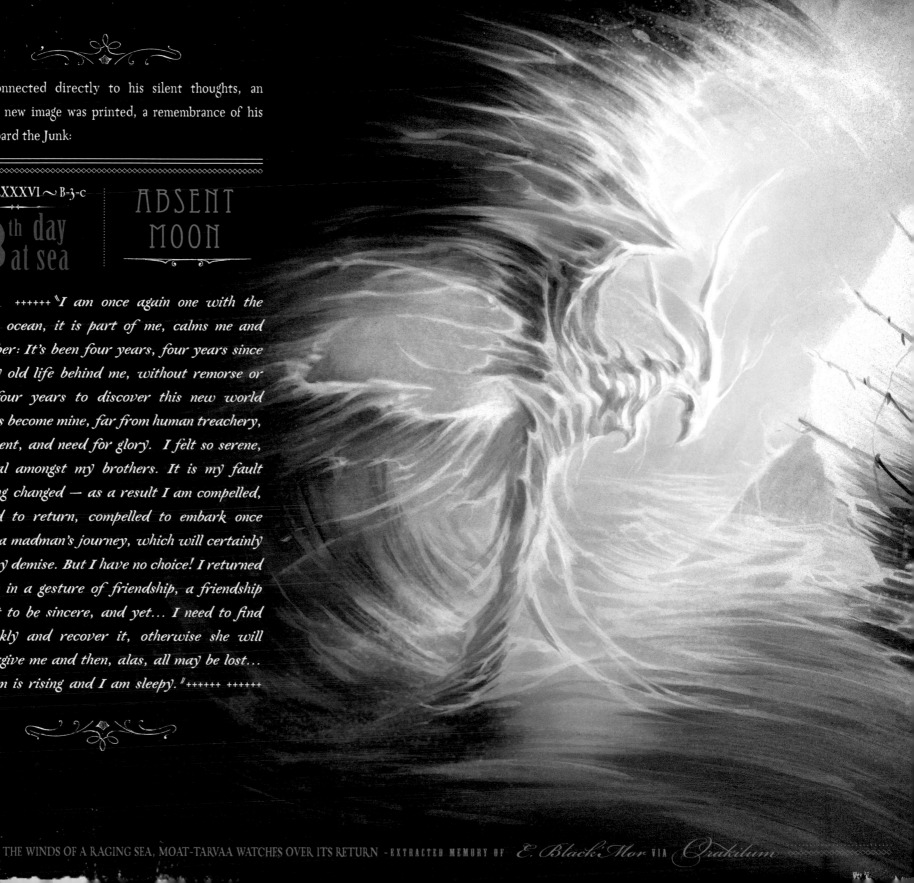

Having connected directly to his silent thoughts, an incredible new image was printed, a remembrance of his return aboard the Junk:

Report CLXXXVI ~ B-3-c

12th day at sea

ABSENT MOON

++++++ "*I am once again one with the ocean, it is part of me, calms me and I remember: It's been four years, four years since I put my old life behind me, without remorse or regret, four years to discover this new world which has become mine, far from human treachery, enslavement, and need for glory. I felt so serene, an animal amongst my brothers. It is my fault everything changed — as a result I am compelled, compelled to return, compelled to embark once again on a madman's journey, which will certainly lead to my demise. But I have no choice! I returned it to him in a gesture of friendship, a friendship I thought to be sincere, and yet... I need to find him quickly and recover it, otherwise she will never forgive me and then, alas, all may be lost... The storm is rising and I am sleepy.*" ++++++ ++++++

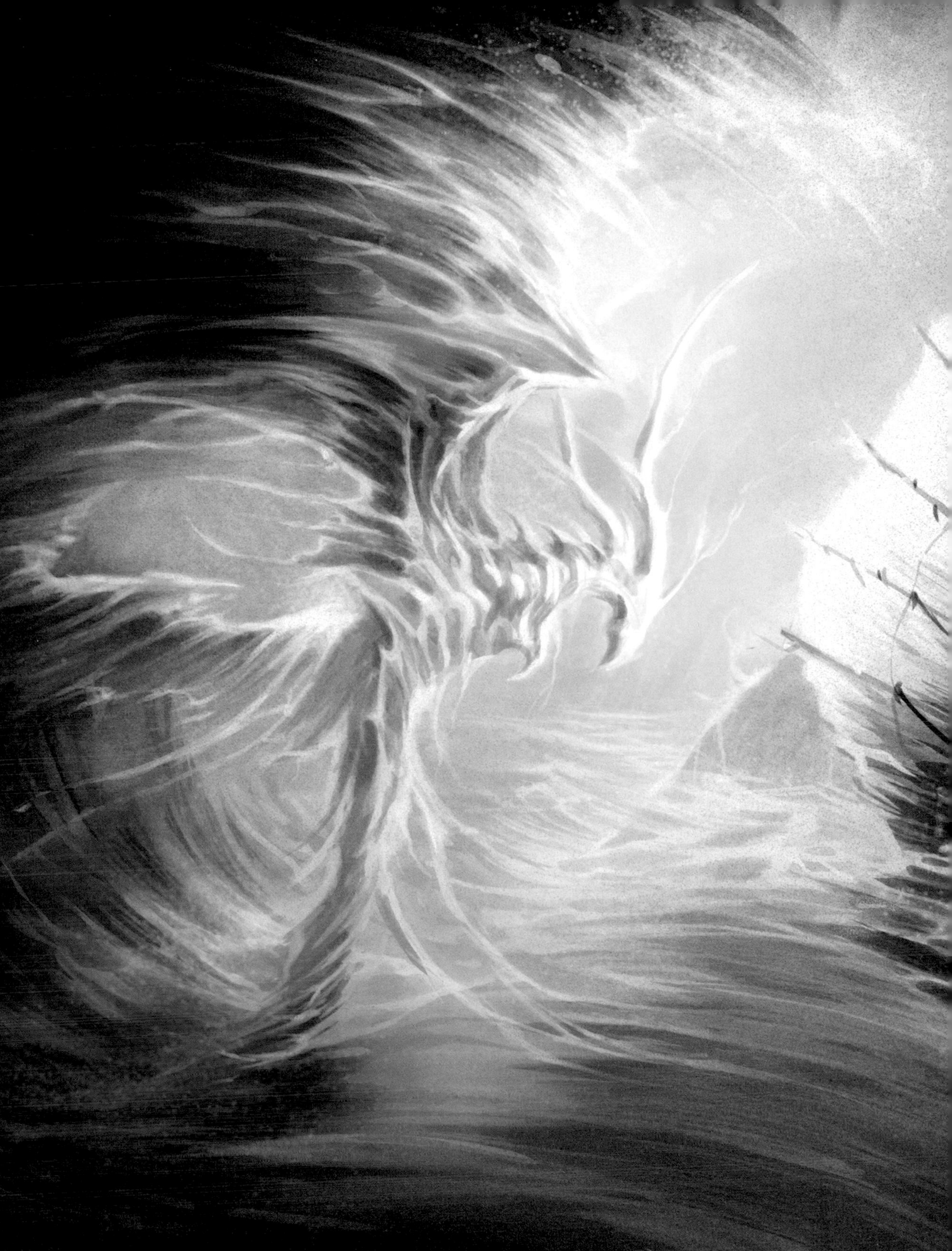

PUSHED BY THE WINDS OF A RAGING SEA, MOAT-TARVAA WATCHES OVER ITS RETURN - EXTRACTED MEMORY OF E. Black'Mor VIA Orakilum

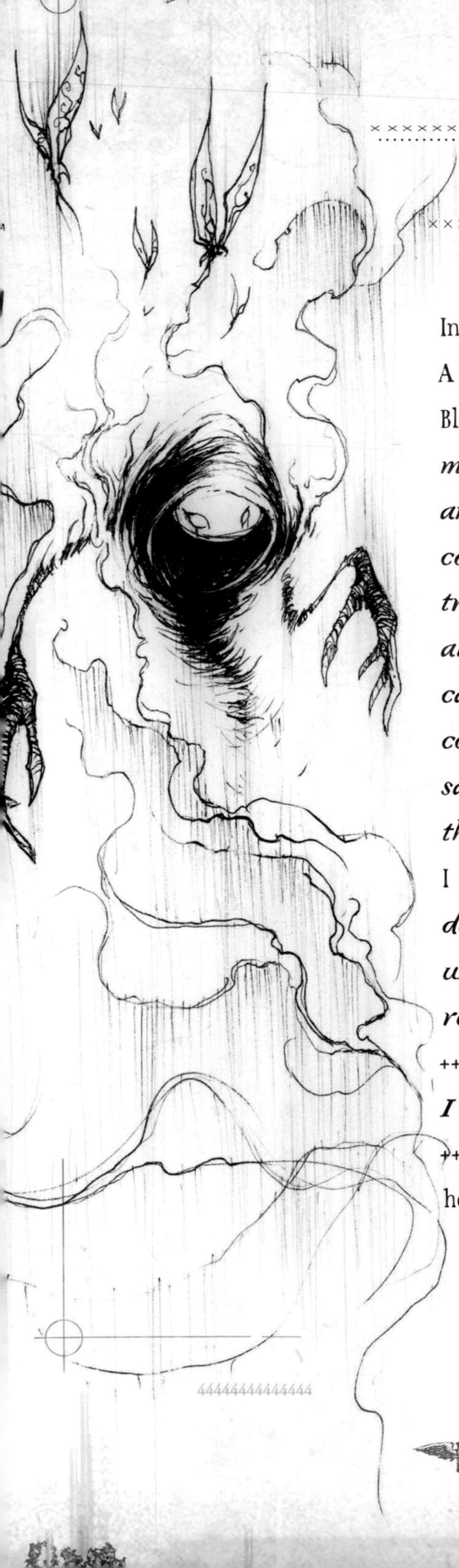

Report CLXXXVI ~ B-3-c

day 05

AN ALCHEMIST'S DREAM

Intrigued, I hastened to ask him: "***Did Pan reveal anything else to you?***"
A silence followed. Then, his stolid gaze fixed on the Northern gate, Black'Mor continued. "***Yes… he showed me my mistake… That terrible misapprehension which started in the Tong brothers' shop in Chengdu and ended at the port of Saigon, when I embarked on the junk of a certain Ma Toshiro under the proud illusion of having uncovered her trafficking. Trafficking… there was no trafficking, because as you already know, it was you she was heading for. My misconception came from others… The learned society to which I had belonged was corrupt from the inside out, right from the start… My learning this sad truth unmasked the senior officials as contemptible members of the Guild of Reapers.***" ++++++ ++++++ ++++++

I leaned toward him to reassure him: "***Indeed, appearances are often deceiving. And I fear it is more difficult nowadays to discern them when we cannot understand all the secrets… Fortunately nothing was revealed to our enemies.***" ++++++

++++++ Nervous, he took off his hat, and continued: "***Unfortunately, as a result, I made a mistake… and it haunts me to this day.***" ++++++ ++++++ ++++++

++++++ I was concerned and encouraged him to continue, but he couldn't find the words, he was too overwrought. I implored him to take a rest.

At that moment the Orakilum knew it had to take over again.

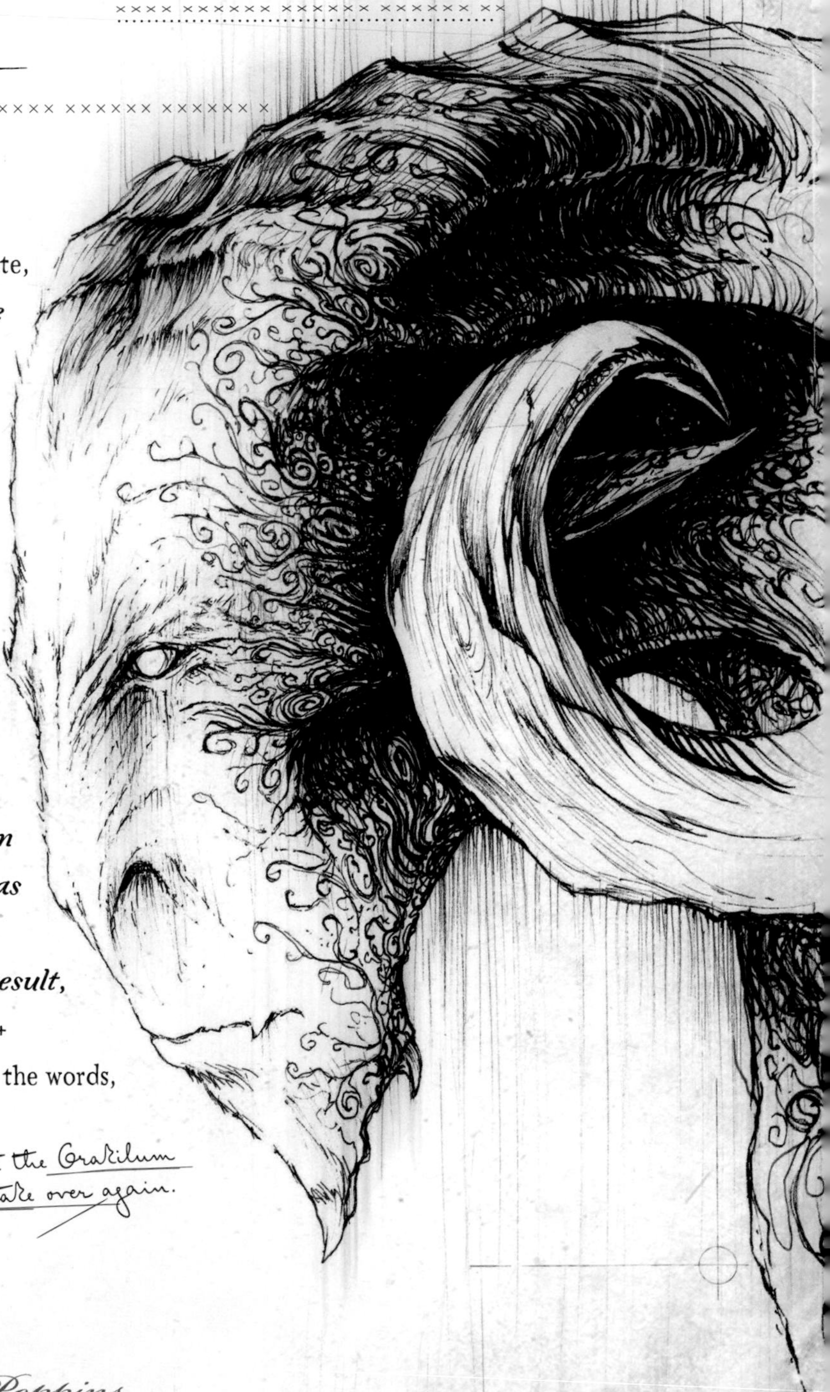

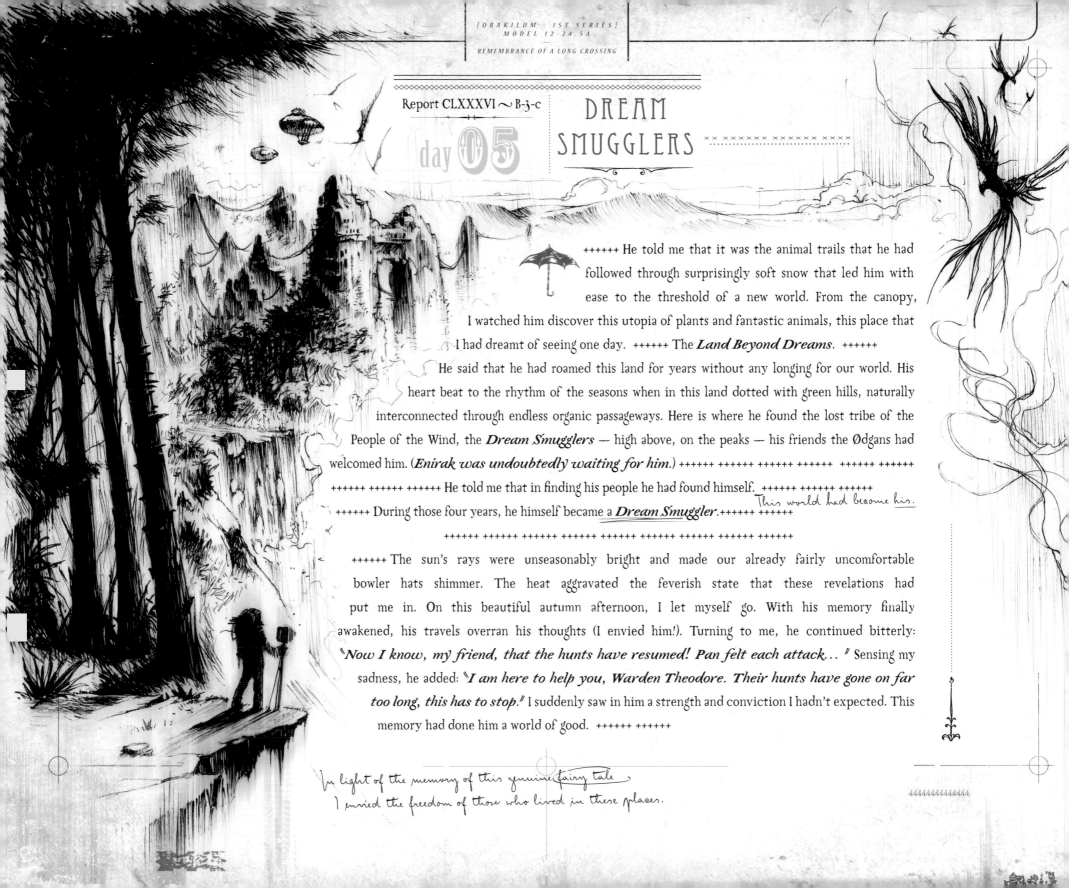

Report CLXXXVI ~ B-3-c

day 05

DREAM SMUGGLERS

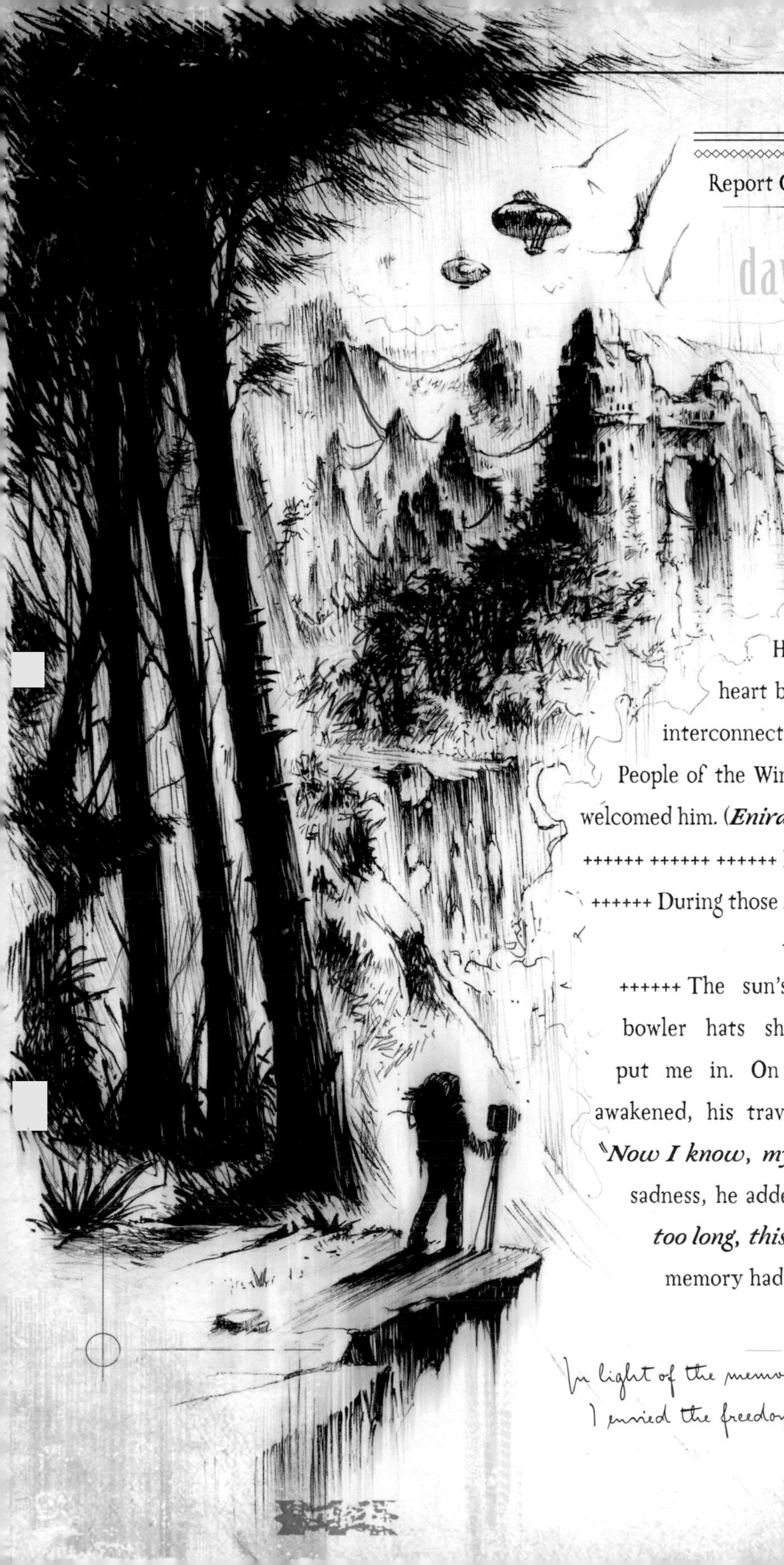

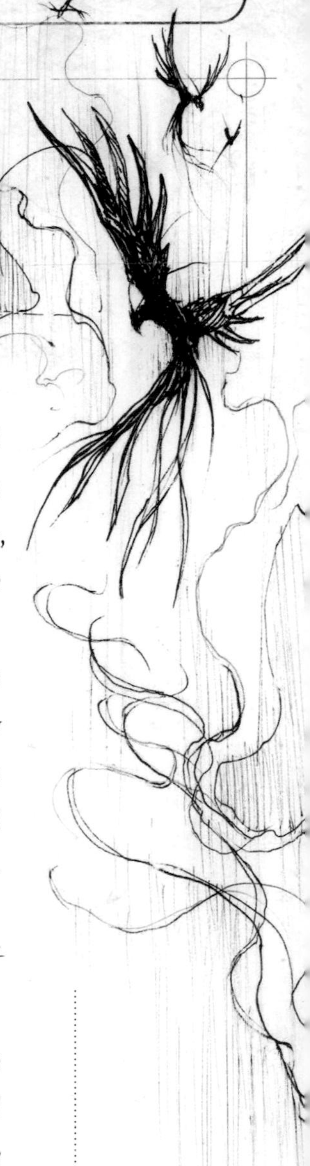

++++++ He told me that it was the animal trails that he had followed through surprisingly soft snow that led him with ease to the threshold of a new world. From the canopy, I watched him discover this utopia of plants and fantastic animals, this place that I had dreamt of seeing one day. ++++++ The ***Land Beyond Dreams***. ++++++

He said that he had roamed this land for years without any longing for our world. His heart beat to the rhythm of the seasons when in this land dotted with green hills, naturally interconnected through endless organic passageways. Here is where he found the lost tribe of the People of the Wind, the ***Dream Smugglers*** — high above, on the peaks — his friends the Ødgans had welcomed him. (***Enirak was undoubtedly waiting for him.***) ++++++ ++++++ ++++++ ++++++ ++++++ ++++++ ++++++ ++++++ ++++++ He told me that in finding his people he had found himself. ++++++ ++++++ ++++++ ++++++ During those four years, he himself became a ***Dream Smuggler***. ++++++ ++++++

This world had become his.

++++++ ++++++ ++++++ ++++++ ++++++ ++++++ ++++++ ++++++ ++++++

++++++ The sun's rays were unseasonably bright and made our already fairly uncomfortable bowler hats shimmer. The heat aggravated the feverish state that these revelations had put me in. On this beautiful autumn afternoon, I let myself go. With his memory finally awakened, his travels overran his thoughts (I envied him!). Turning to me, he continued bitterly: "***Now I know, my friend, that the hunts have resumed! Pan felt each attack…***" Sensing my sadness, he added: "***I am here to help you, Warden Theodore. Their hunts have gone on far too long, this has to stop.***" I suddenly saw in him a strength and conviction I hadn't expected. This memory had done him a world of good. ++++++ ++++++

In light of the memory of this genuine fairy tale
I envied the freedom of those who lived in these places.

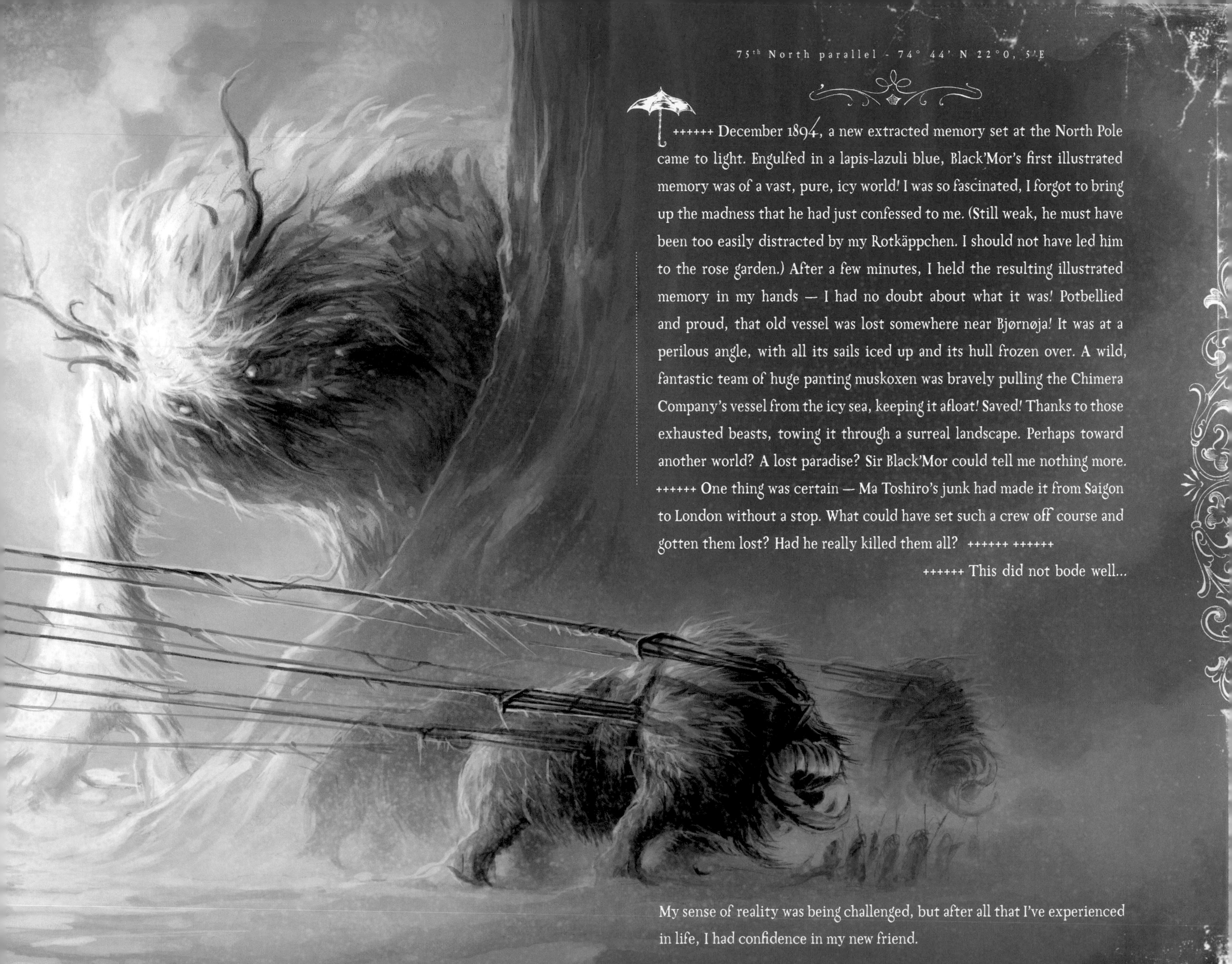

T++++++ December 1894, a new extracted memory set at the North Pole came to light. Engulfed in a lapis-lazuli blue, Black'Mor's first illustrated memory was of a vast, pure, icy world! I was so fascinated, I forgot to bring up the madness that he had just confessed to me. (Still weak, he must have been too easily distracted by my Rotkäppchen. I should not have led him to the rose garden.) After a few minutes, I held the resulting illustrated memory in my hands — I had no doubt about what it was! Potbellied and proud, that old vessel was lost somewhere near Bjørnøja! It was at a perilous angle, with all its sails iced up and its hull frozen over. A wild, fantastic team of huge panting muskoxen was bravely pulling the Chimera Company's vessel from the icy sea, keeping it afloat! Saved! Thanks to those exhausted beasts, towing it through a surreal landscape. Perhaps toward another world? A lost paradise? Sir Black'Mor could tell me nothing more. ++++++ One thing was certain — Ma Toshiro's junk had made it from Saigon to London without a stop. What could have set such a crew off course and gotten them lost? Had he really killed them all? ++++++ ++++++

++++++ This did not bode well...

My sense of reality was being challenged, but after all that I've experienced in life, I had confidence in my new friend.

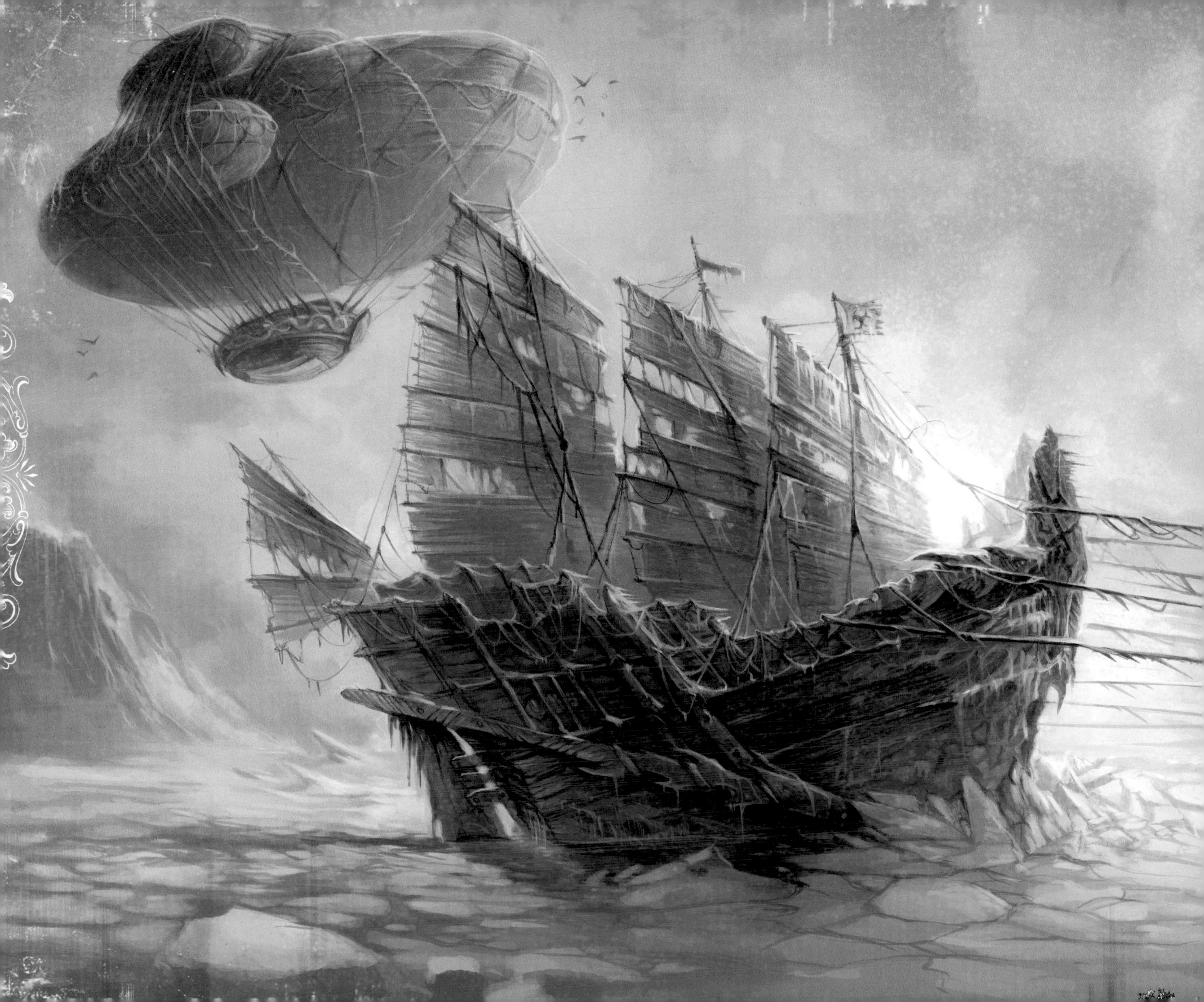

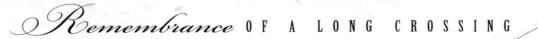

Remembrance OF A LONG CROSSING

Report CLXXXVI ~ B-3-c

46TH file

FROM THE YEAR 1899

FEAR

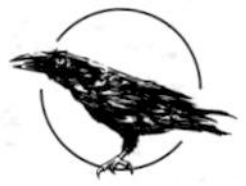

00 UMBRELLA 'POPS'

STORY OF A ROUND TRIP

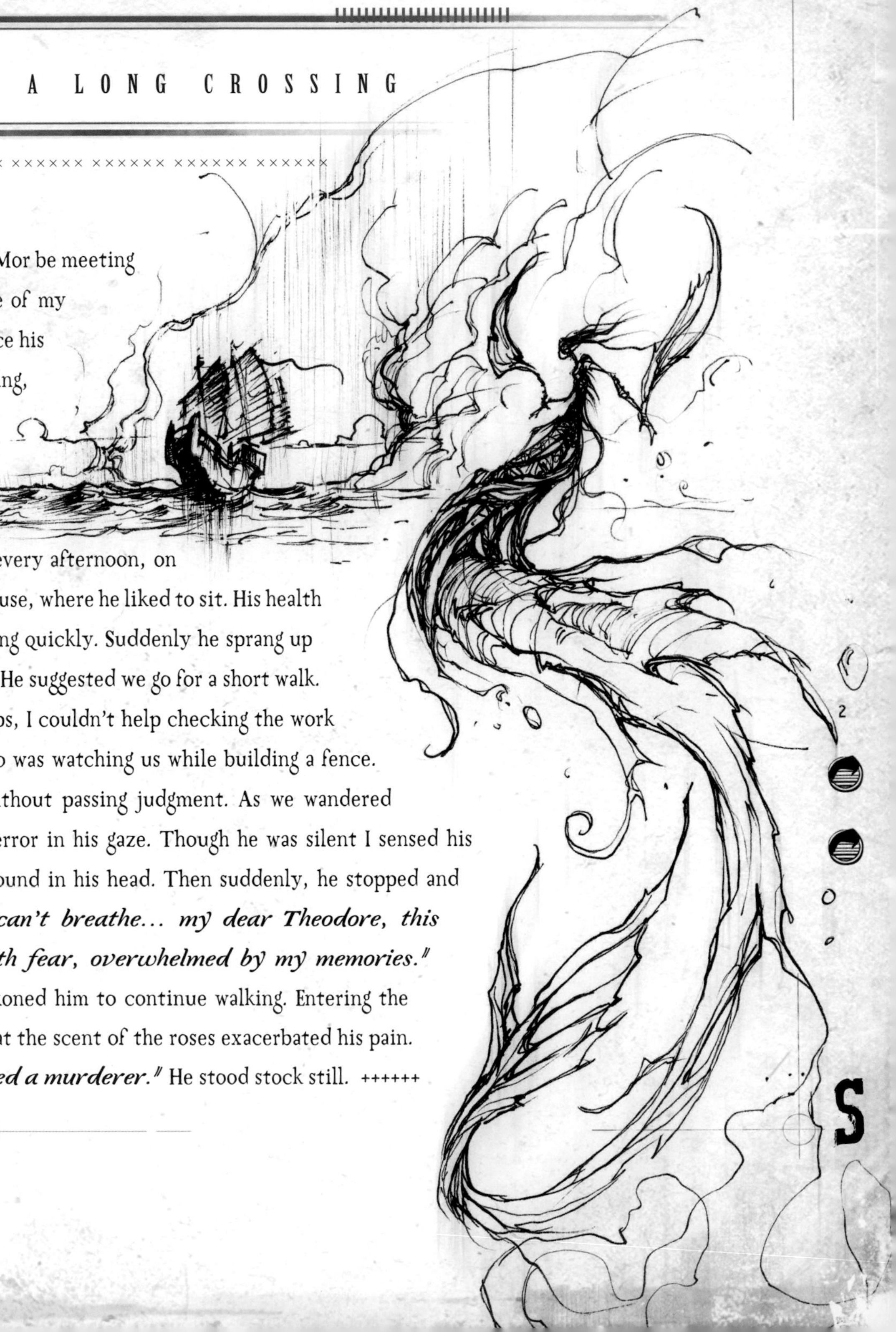

++++++ Who could Sir Elian Black'Mor be meeting on this bench hidden in the middle of my Park? About a month had passed since his revival, and inevitably, he was waiting, but for what? A response? A person? Peace?

I found him, as I did at the end of every afternoon, on the northern path below the greenhouse, where he liked to sit. His health was still fragile, but he was recovering quickly. Suddenly he sprang up off the bench. His face was feverish. He suggested we go for a short walk. He seemed agitated. After a few steps, I couldn't help checking the work of the young centaur Filzadius, who was watching us while building a fence. My lodgers accepted his arrival without passing judgment. As we wandered the pathways I couldn't miss the terror in his gaze. Though he was silent I sensed his confusion; words were bouncing around in his head. Then suddenly, he stopped and admitted, "***I'm frightened... I can't breathe... my dear Theodore, this evening my heart is racing with fear, overwhelmed by my memories.***" As a friend, without a word, I beckoned him to continue walking. Entering the rose garden, I got the impression that the scent of the roses exacerbated his pain. "***I left as a stowaway and arrived a murderer.***" He stood stock still. ++++++

S

4444444444444

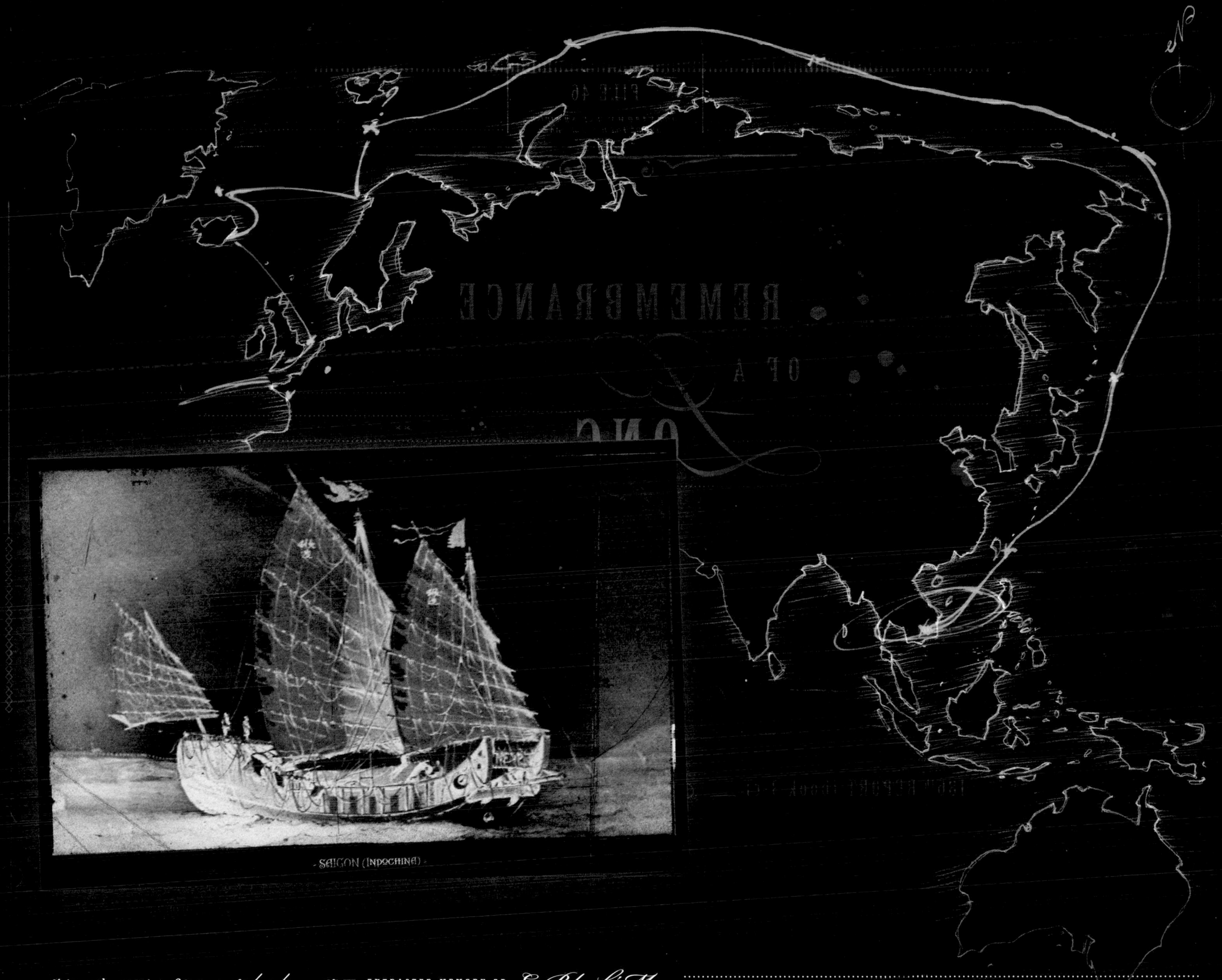
N
- SAIGON (INDOCHINE) -

xx xxxxxxx x —*Saigon, the morning of Oct. 19, 1894, 5:41 a.m. GMT* - EXTRACTED MEMORY OF *E. Black'Mor*

46TH FILE

[ORAKILUM : 1ST SERIES]
MODEL 12 - 24.5A

REMEMBRANCE OF A LONG CROSSING 1894-1899

186th REPORT {book 3-c} __ *Somewhere in the middle of nowhere*

4

8-7-72

MEMORY OF SHADOWS, OCT. 31, 1899 - 3:00 AM - GMT

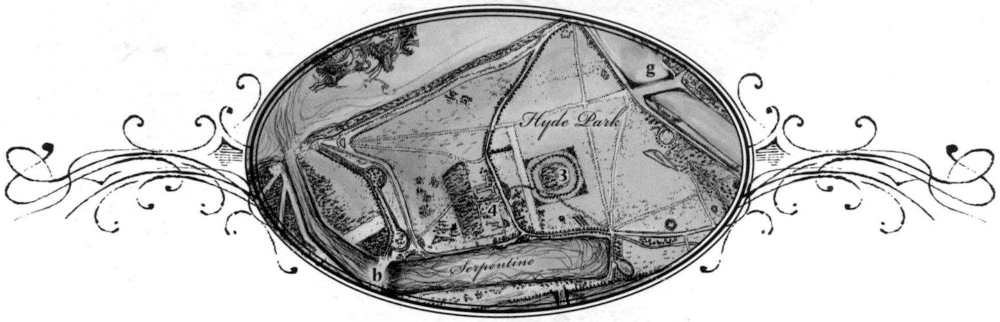
Hyde Park
g
3
4
b
Serpentine

3 Bandstand - 4 Little Theatre - b Bridge - g Gateway

++++++ I stared at this man, deathly pale yet still alive! ++++++ ++++++ Since his arrival, his face — a picture of lethargy — had invaded my nights. When we first exchanged glances, we seemed to recognize one another; his image appeared sharper, more familiar. I was disconcerted... I also forgot the most basic of courtesies, to introduce myself. When it was done, he smiled at me. "***Thank you kindly for the rabbit's foot, Sir Theodore Jolicœur Poppins,***" he murmured. ++++++ "***If my memory is not playing tricks on me, my name is Black'Mor, Elian Black'Mor, and you have saved my life! I will be forever grateful.***" ++++++

++++++ Seeing that he was a little dazed from his first contact with the Orakilum, I decided to leave it at that, content that he had retained his good humor. ++++++ ++++++ ++++++ ++++++

++++++ I end this report relieved, as you should be. [...] ++++++ Sharing my Samhain civet pudding should perk him up. ++++++

++++++ Before approving this 46th file, please take into account the fact that upon the arrival of his (as you clearly know, long-awaited) ***Sylvilagus transitionalis***, the machine had suddenly — and for the first time ever — acted of its own free will. Strangely, this had never happened before in forty-nine years of use. (???)

END OF REPORT ON RHAPSODY OF THE SHADOWS

—HYDE PARK ++++++

SAMHAIN, OCT. 31, 1899 - 00 P.M. - GMT

REVIVAL

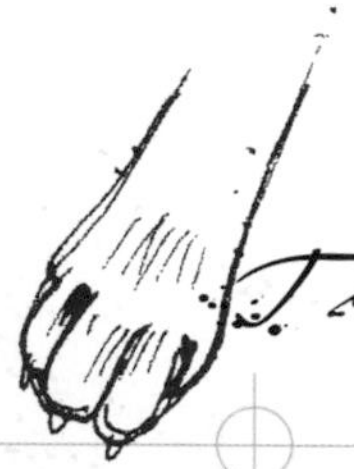

Theodore P

(Could you please promptly inform me of my new instructions?)

2

4444444444444

++++++

"*Falling asleep at the ends of the earth,*
in the middle of nowhere,
to wake up at the Gate of Dreams.

++++++

It all seemed impossible,
or even unimaginable,
and yet…"

++++++ ++++++ ++++++

2^B

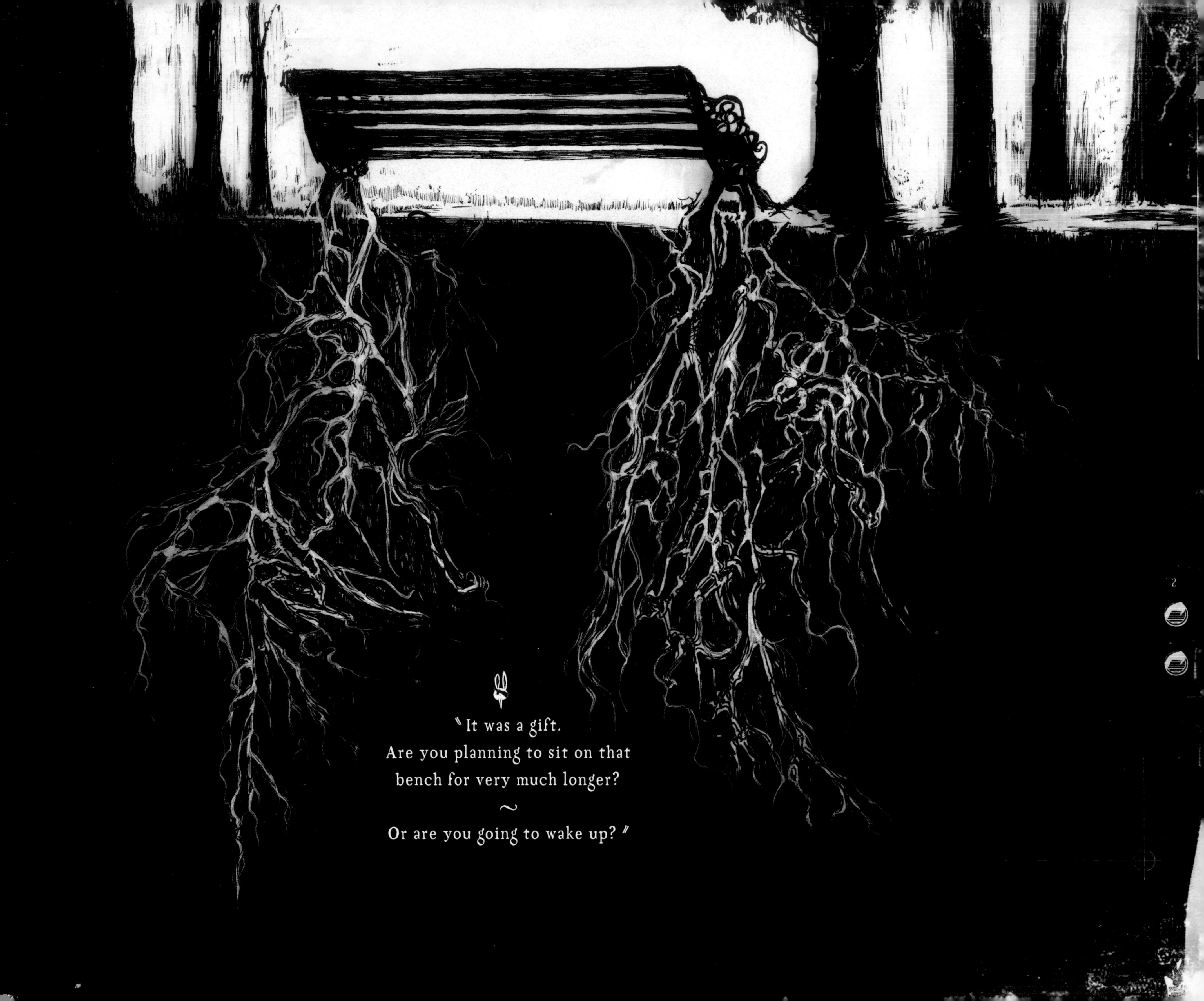

"It was a gift.
Are you planning to sit on that
bench for very much longer?
~
Or are you going to wake up?"

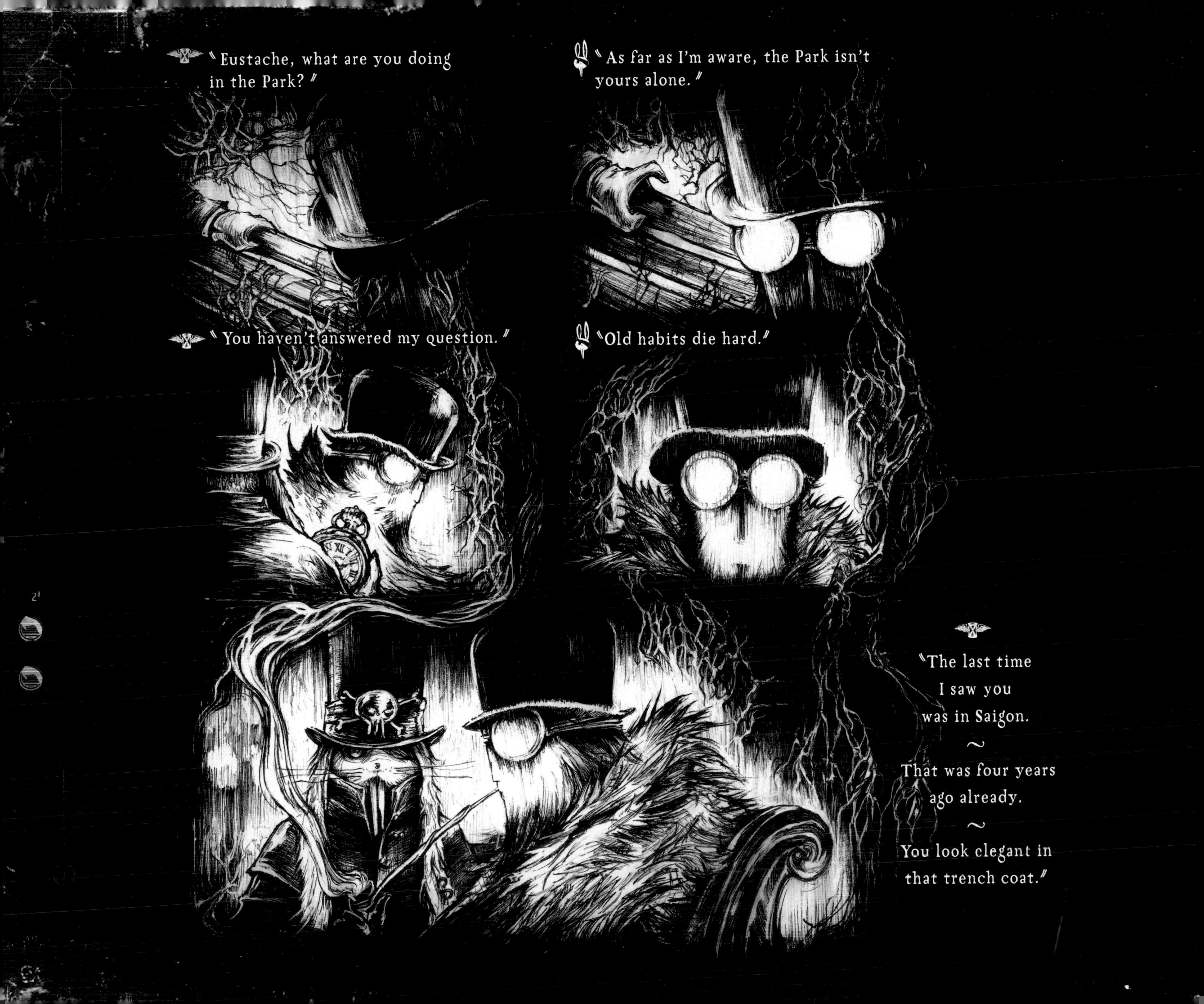
"Eustache, what are you doing in the Park?"
"As far as I'm aware, the Park isn't yours alone."
"You haven't answered my question."
"Old habits die hard."
"The last time I saw you was in Saigon.
~
That was four years ago already.
~
You look elegant in that trench coat."

TICK - TOCK
TICK - TOCK
TICK - TOCK
TICK - TOCK
TICK - TOCK
TICK - TOCK TICK - TOCK TOCK
TICK - TOCK TICK - TOCK TOCK
TICK - TOCK, TICK - TOCK TOCK VISUAL MEMORY
TICK - TOCK

Orakiline

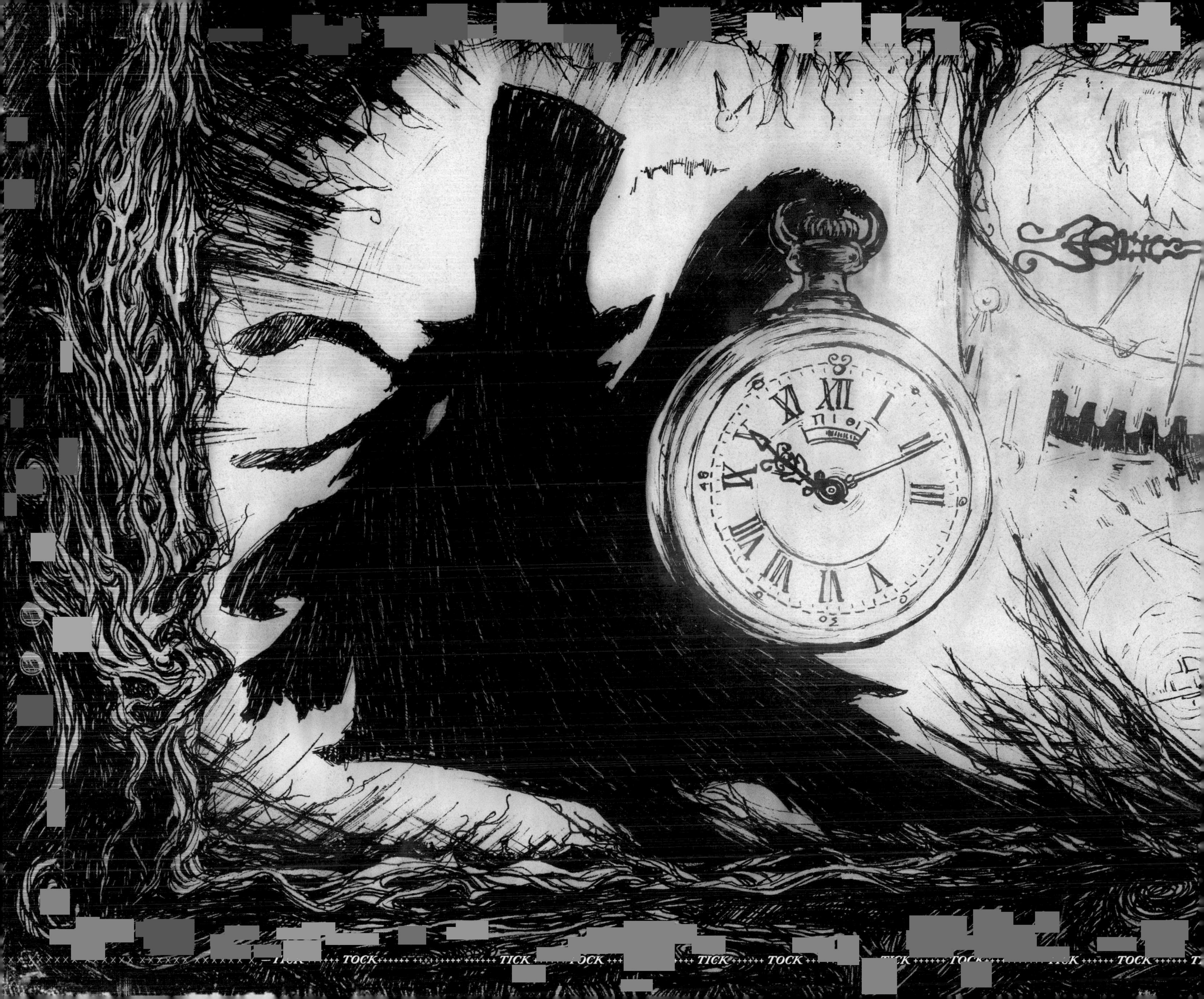
TICK ++++++ TOCK

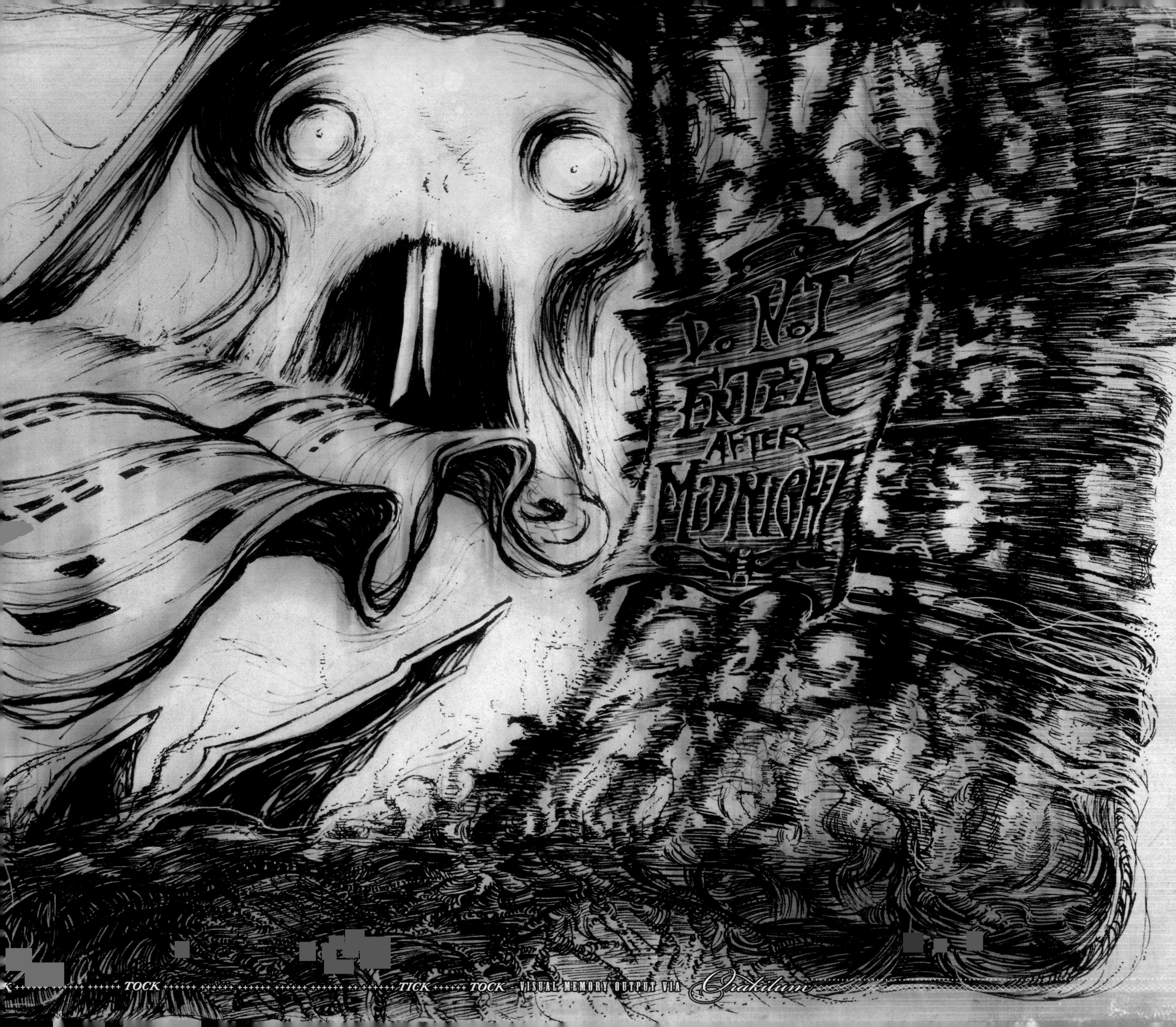
DO NOT ENTER AFTER MIDNIGHT
TOCK ++++++ TICK ++++++ TOCK VISUAL MEMORY OUTPUT VIA Orakilum
2

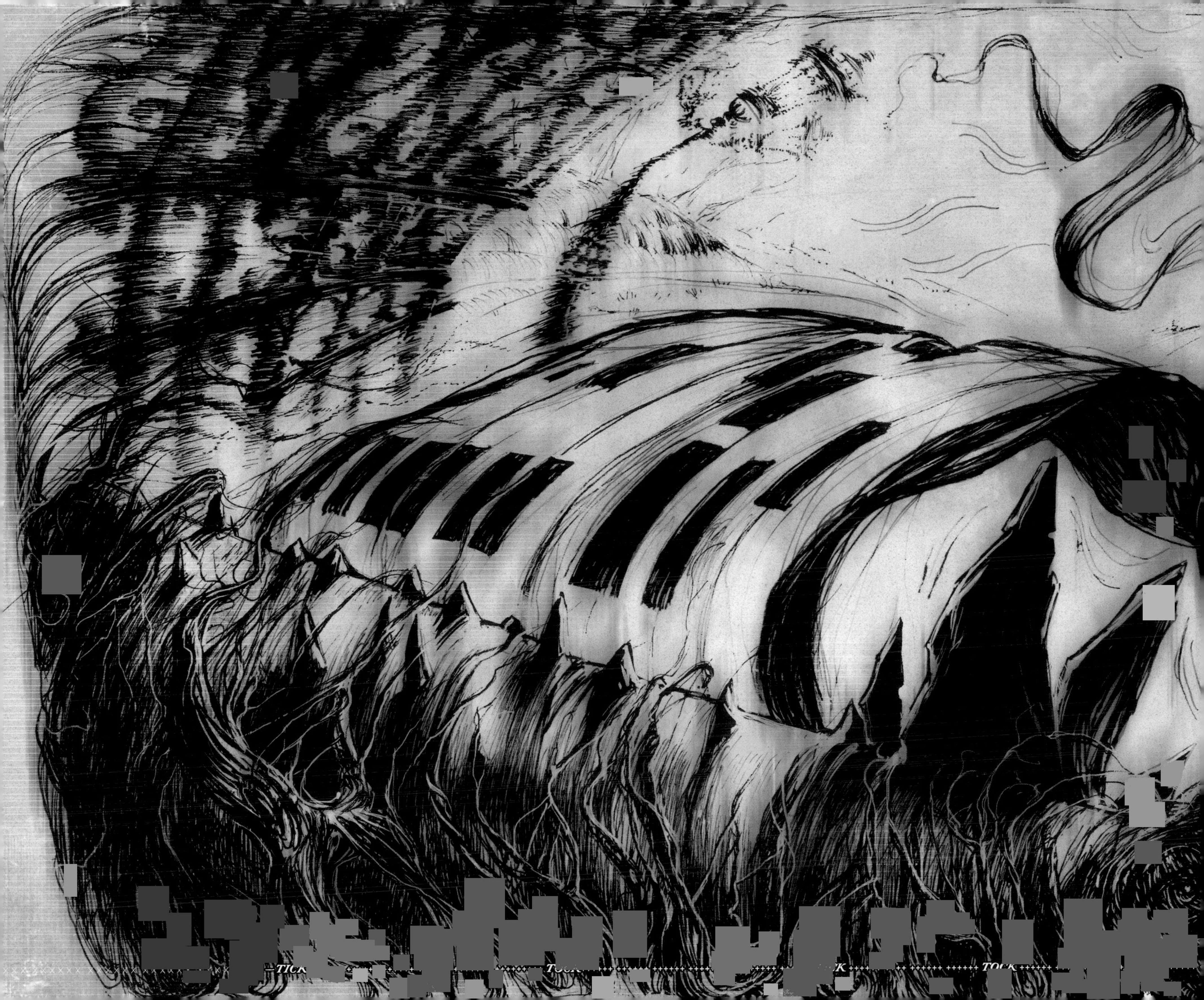
TICK
TOCK
TOCK

memory of shadows

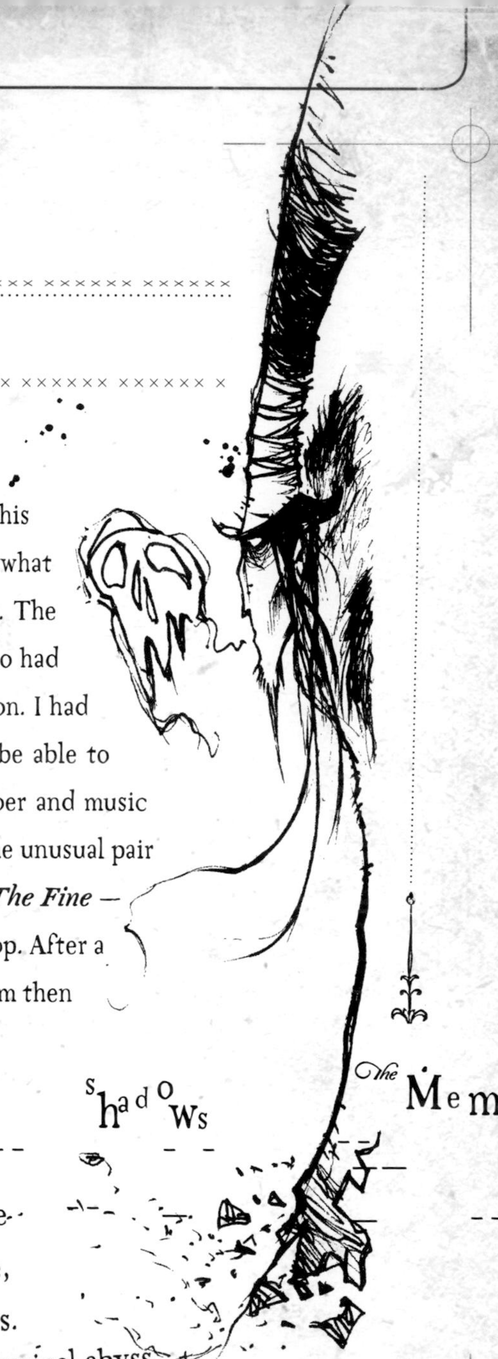

Report CLXXXV ∼ B-3-a

day 11

THE SEPULCHRAL DUO
ON THE NIGHT OF SAMHAIN
— *Hyde Park, evening of Oct 31, 1899,*
EXTRACTED MEMORY OF
T. Poppins

++++++ This morning, the sound of my alarm clock was accompanied by a sweet melody. This mesmerizing chant resonated through the early morning fog, and I clearly saw (and understood) what was going to play out today. The whole Park was already humming their mesmerizing refrains. The fantastic Victorian-rock duo, *The Memory of Shadows,* was back. These two musicians, who had died 99 years ago almost to the day, had prepared a special sepulchral concert for the occasion. I had to pinch myself. WOOOOW! It was suddenly all so simple, so obvious. I was finally going to be able to lure the one who didn't want to come. I was sure of it now. I knew that as an avid concertgoer and music lover, my dear old Eustache could not resist this. Without any further ado, I caught up with the unusual pair — the appropriately named bass player, *Little Finger,* and his sidekick, the organgrinder *Roby The Fine* — and asked them to put the impossible to music... Rabbi Loew's Formula Vitae in a recurring loop. After a brief look at the formula, they agreed and without further ado, started playing what would from then on be known as *"The Rhapsody of the Shadows."*

The Memory of shadows *The* Memory of shadows *The* Memory of shadows

From Undines to our brother wolves, including the Faun, every one of the lodgers listened, lulled by the soothing effect of this music from beyond the grave, this slow descent into a musical abyss.

MUSICAL ABYSS - MUSICAL ABYSS - ABYSS - Abyss musical abyss
MUSICAL ABYSS MUSICAL ABYSS

Melodies of shadows - shadows shadows

BURROW - LOST soul - LOST
VOID - black hole - leporid - MUSICAL VISIT -
LEPORID BURROW

Under the effects of their Art, I've lost all control of the Orakilum! (?). It started to do its own thing, independent of my will, as though it too were possessed. Other than that little detail everything else seemed to be fine. I can't seem to get it back under my control. I'll just have to wait.

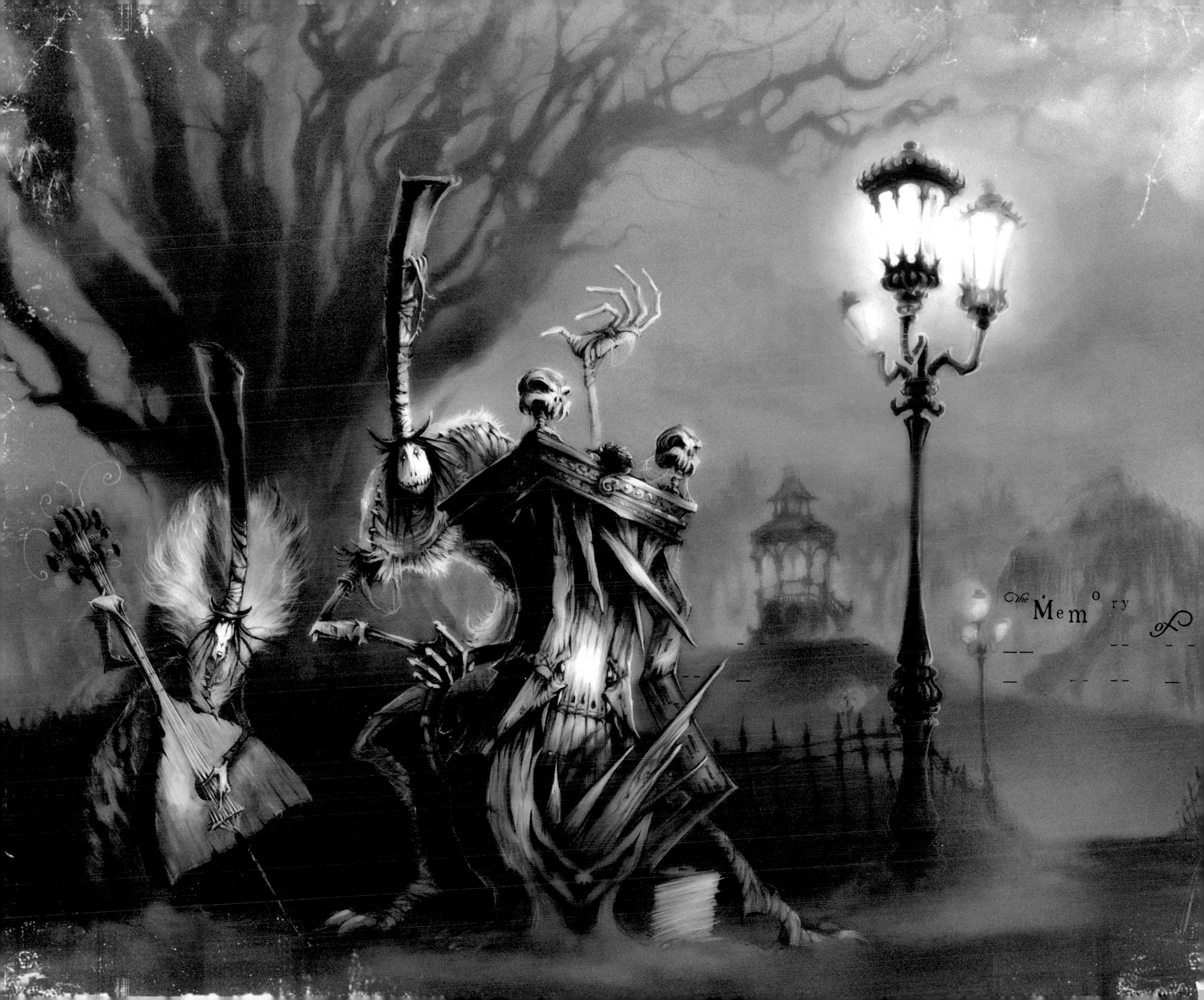
The Memory of

The Rhapsody OF SHADOWS

Report CLXXXV ∼ B-3-a

46ᵀᴴ file

FROM THE YEAR 1899

THE SLEEPER

3 UMBRELLA 'POPS'

THE WHITE RABBIT COMES TO THE ARBORETUM

 ++++++ Honorable Members of the Order of Architects, I have a confession to make. On this night of October 1899, I am having doubts about our joint decision to keep him buried in the Park. Do you not think that this land, no longer his own, is deliberately keeping him alive but unconscious, almost as though it were protecting him? For two seasons now he has worn the mask of life, yet one would think him dead and *"the burrow of the Cursed"* seems devoid of all Leporids.

++++++ It's completely incomprehensible! ++++++

++++++ I should just shrug it off, but this new lodger is obsessing me, haunting me. From my Guardhouse, I can see the Dragon turning around this dormant tomb every hour of every day, like a tortured soul. Sometimes, I feel reassured watching this lodger, inert, sleeping for all eternity. But how do you wake up those who are not actually asleep? How do you call those who do not want to come?

++++++ My attention should be focused elsewhere as the first autumn leaves are already trembling, and I know that the hunts will soon resume. I have already counted over one hundred and ninety creatures who have found sanctuary here. How many more will come this winter?

I fear the consequences of our choices.

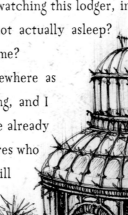
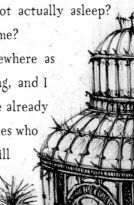

A little music accompanied by some "Blue London" would do me wonders, if only. . . .

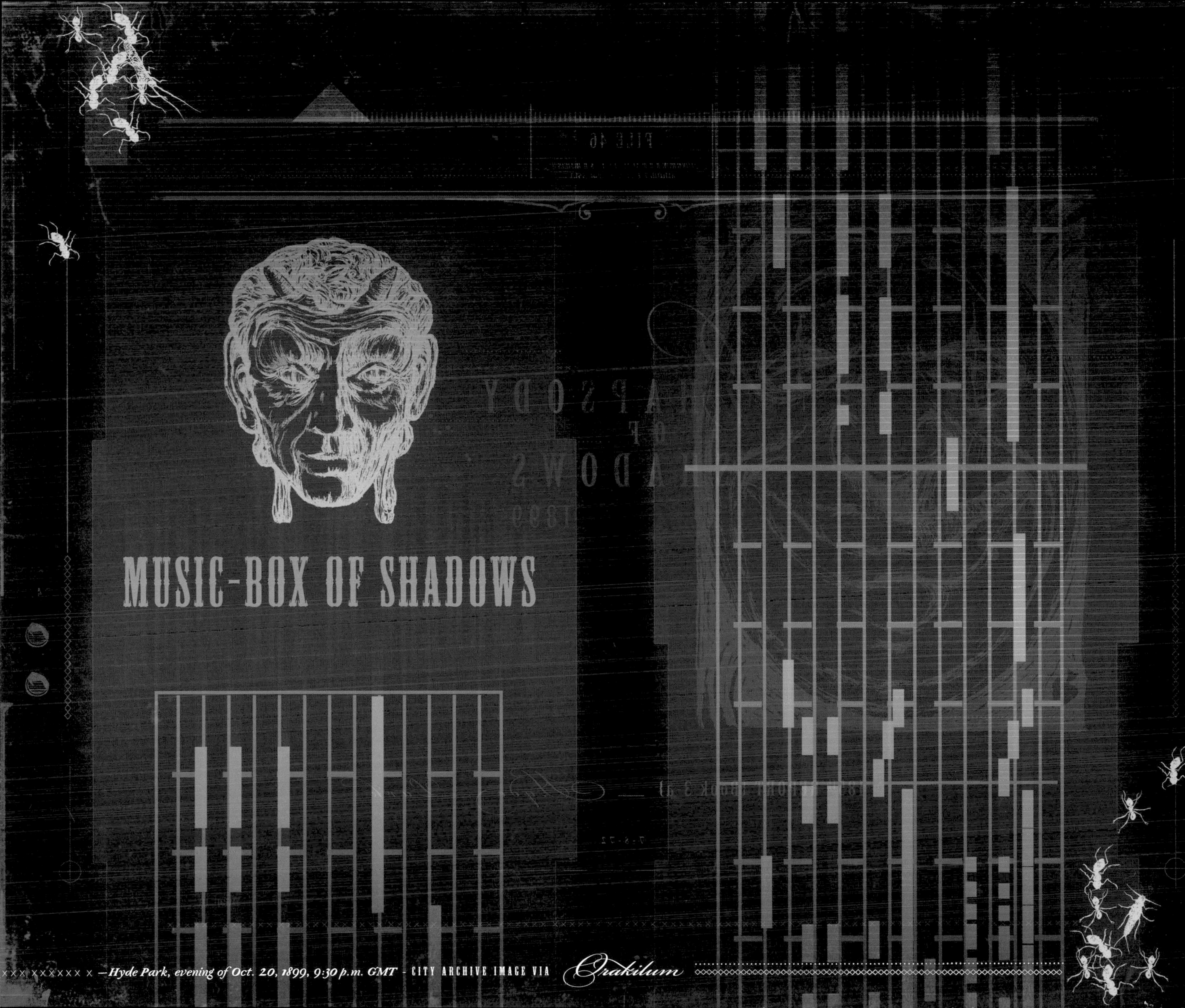
MUSIC-BOX OF SHADOWS
xxx xxxxxxx x —Hyde Park, evening of Oct. 20, 1899, 9:30 p.m. GMT - CITY ARCHIVE IMAGE VIA Orakilum

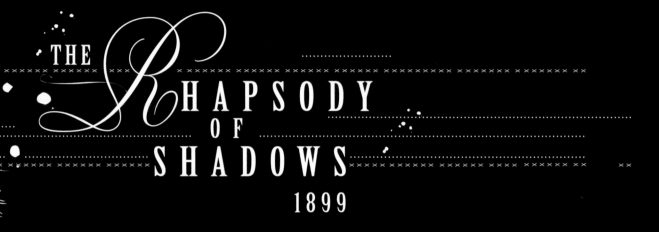

46TH FILE

[ORAKILUM : 1ST SERIES]
MODEL 12 - 24.5A

THE RHAPSODY OF SHADOWS

1899

4

185th REPORT {Book 3-a} — Hyde Park

8-7-72

IIIIOII III

THE UNDINES, DEC. 29, 1898 · 4:00 A.M. GMT

Report CLXXXIII ~ B-2-a

day 13

A CARING FRIEND

Serpentine
Island
b
10
Dark Water
Kew Gardens
b
b
14
15
16

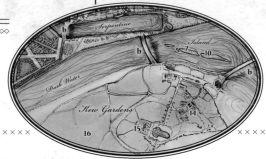

7 Infirmary - 10 Nursery
14 Stables
15 Palm House
16 Domain of the Wild
b Bridges

++++++ My new lodger had been sleeping at the bottom of their freshwater pool for several days. The Undines were taking care of him. Oddly enough it seemed that their voices, their songs, held him there, clinging to our world. ++++++ I was fascinated.++++++ Muffled and melancholic, their laughter resonated through the Kew Gardens greenhouse! ++++++

++++++ They laughed and laughed, mocking me more and more each day! I got the feeling that they didn't want to give him back to me. They loved that body, and had charmed it to the point… ~~I do believe~~ it seemed … of being loved back.

++++++ That's why, the moment when the last root untwined itself from the soaking body, my stomach was in knots. I would have to get them to see reason! And I have to admit — those of you who know them will understand — that the thought of it did not thrill me. ++++++ I hesitated but yet I had to act. ++++++

++++++ Finally, his traveling (winged!) companion helped in his own way ~ the shadow of his majestic flight frightened them away. Each time he came near I noticed that they were scared of him. ++++++ I only had an instant, a split second, to pull the unraveled body away from those black widows. If I hadn't been quick, I would have fallen prey and would have been, believe you me, lying next to him, drowned. (Let's hope that they won't hold a grudge.) they most likely will!!!

++++++ ++++++ ++++++ ++++++ Now that his body was finally free from the vines that had nurtured him during his amazing journey, he was liberated. His vital signs appeared normal, and all that was left was a combination of black symbols, scars, prominent on his left forearm. However, as we had feared during our last exchange, I cannot say the same for his soul. It seemed absent, still dormant. ++++++ ++++++ ++++++ +++++

01/11/1899 01:36

I took him to my personal Arboretum, where arrangements had been made. His ***white rabbit**** was for him. Together, they were supposed to take the sinuous path back to the land of men. ++++++ ***That way madness lay.***

*I just hope that this time, for once, he won't be too late. 2

END OF THE REPORT ON THE RETURN OF AN OLD FRIEND

—PALM HOUSE ++++++

AWAKENING, JAN. 11, 1899 - 1 A.M. GMT

CONFIDENTIAL

Theodore P

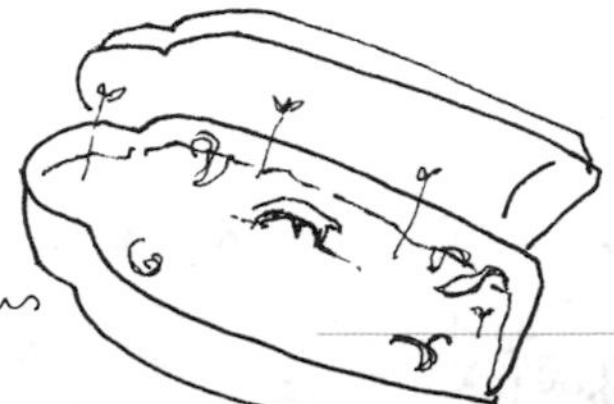

I am still curious about where the sarcophagus came from.

4444444444444

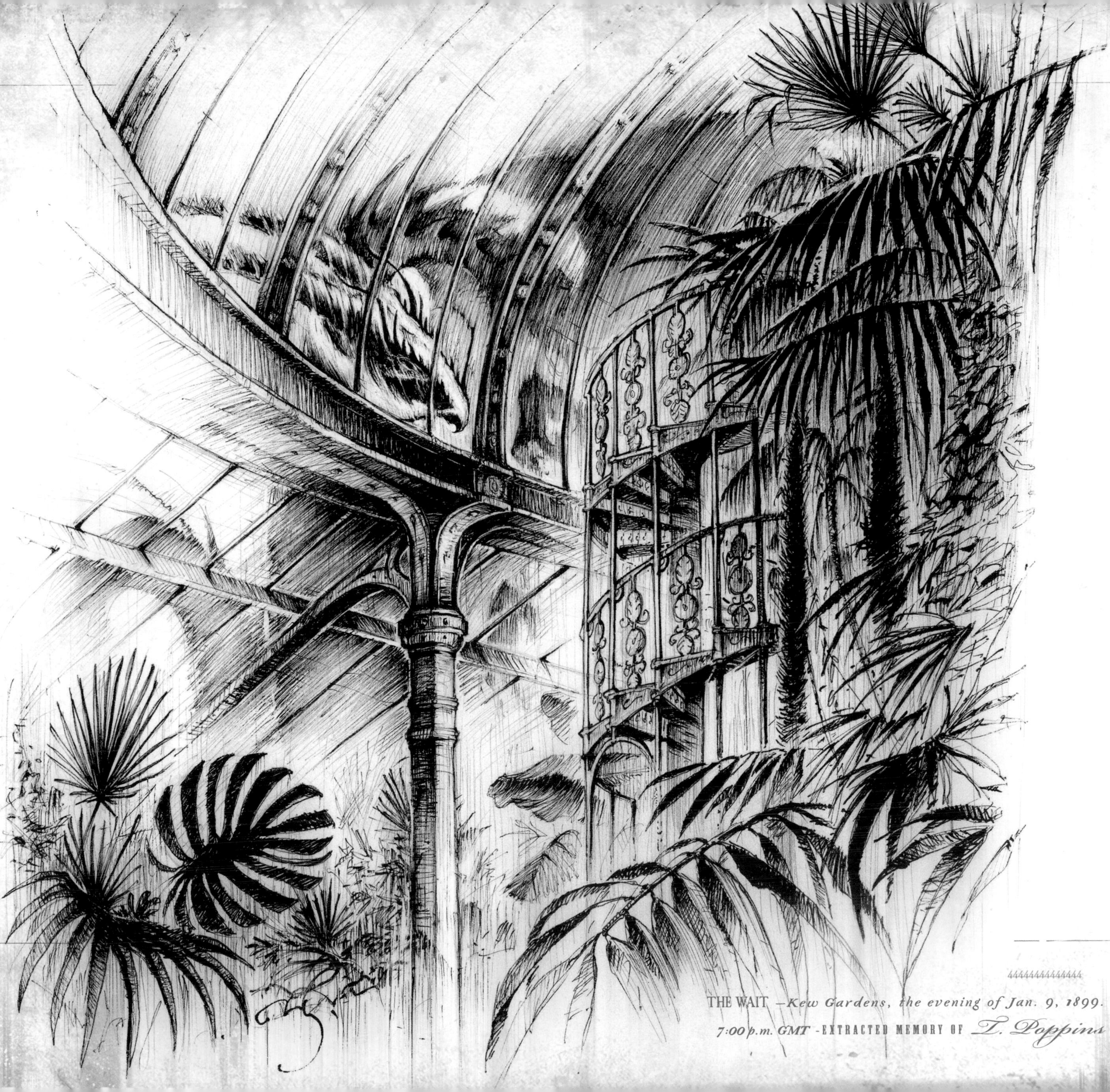

THE WAIT –*Kew Gardens, the evening of Jan. 9, 1899.*
7:00 p.m. GMT -EXTRACTED MEMORY OF *T. Poppins*

Report CLXXX ~ B-2-a

day 02

TEARS OF THE UNDINES

++++++ *"Guardian angels, I desperately need your help!"* I did not even get a ripple in response to my call. Unable to wait any longer, I placed the carefully closed sarcophagus into their pool. It sank straightaway and lay in the shadows of the giant water lilies. Since I had acted without having waited or made an offering, I was fearful of their wrath... *"Undines, please excuse the intrusion! My actions are in no way meant to offend. This sarcophagus was turning to dust in my powerless hands! I couldn't wait any longer! I am sure you understand."* I was fully aware that my words could all be in vain... Undines are particularly sensitive... ++++++ A piercing look cut through the marbled water.

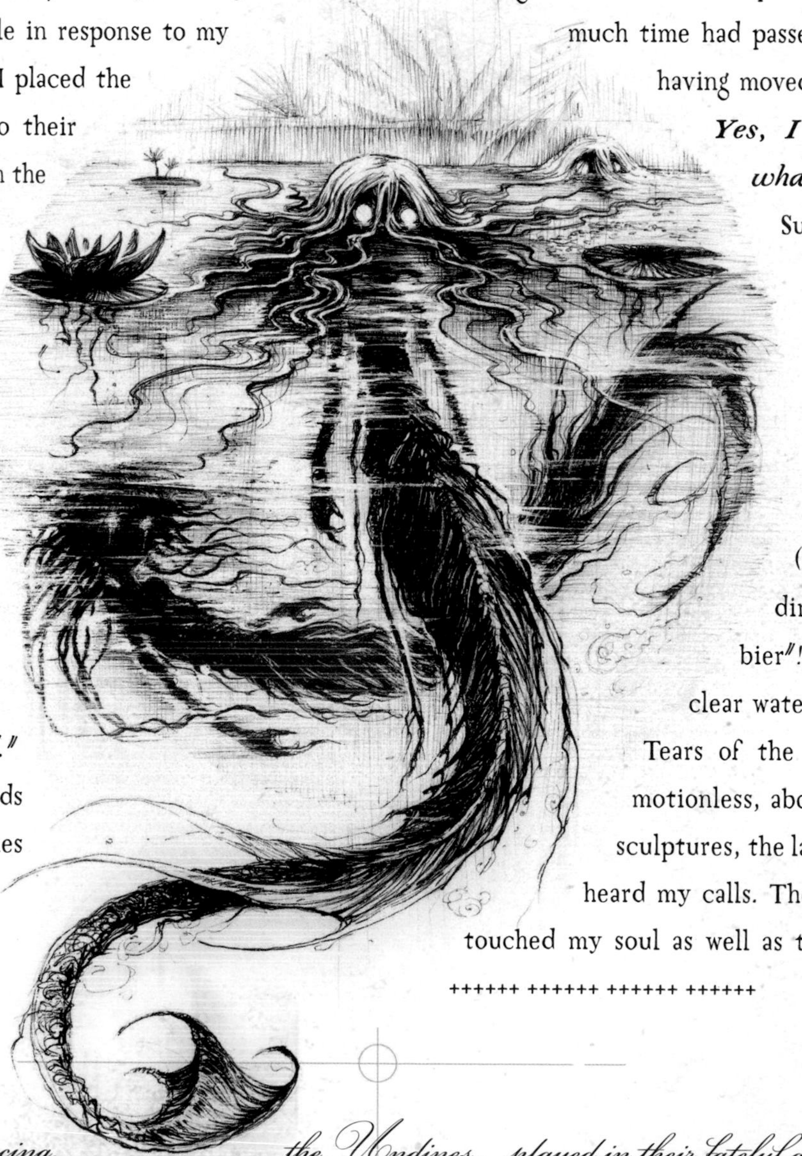

Sitting on the side of the pool, I became frightened as too much time had passed without any of the three having moved. *"Yes, I did offend you. Yes, I fear your wrath! But what other choice did I have?"* Suddenly I felt an icy wind fill the space. The shadow of the Dragon, which had been relentlessly circling overhead since I had slipped the "casket" into the water, had just landed. The beast (worried?) had fixed its claws directly above the "watery bier"! Suddenly, I saw trickles of clear water fall from their closed eyes. Tears of the Undines. Unbelievably sad, motionless, above the waters, these surreal sculptures, the last sirens of the streams, had heard my calls. The appearance of their elixir touched my soul as well as the entangled body... ++++++

++++++ ++++++ ++++++ ++++++

Lively, swaying, dancing, the Undines played in their fateful aquatic ring, laughing in the safety of their freshwater pool.

I am aware of the danger.

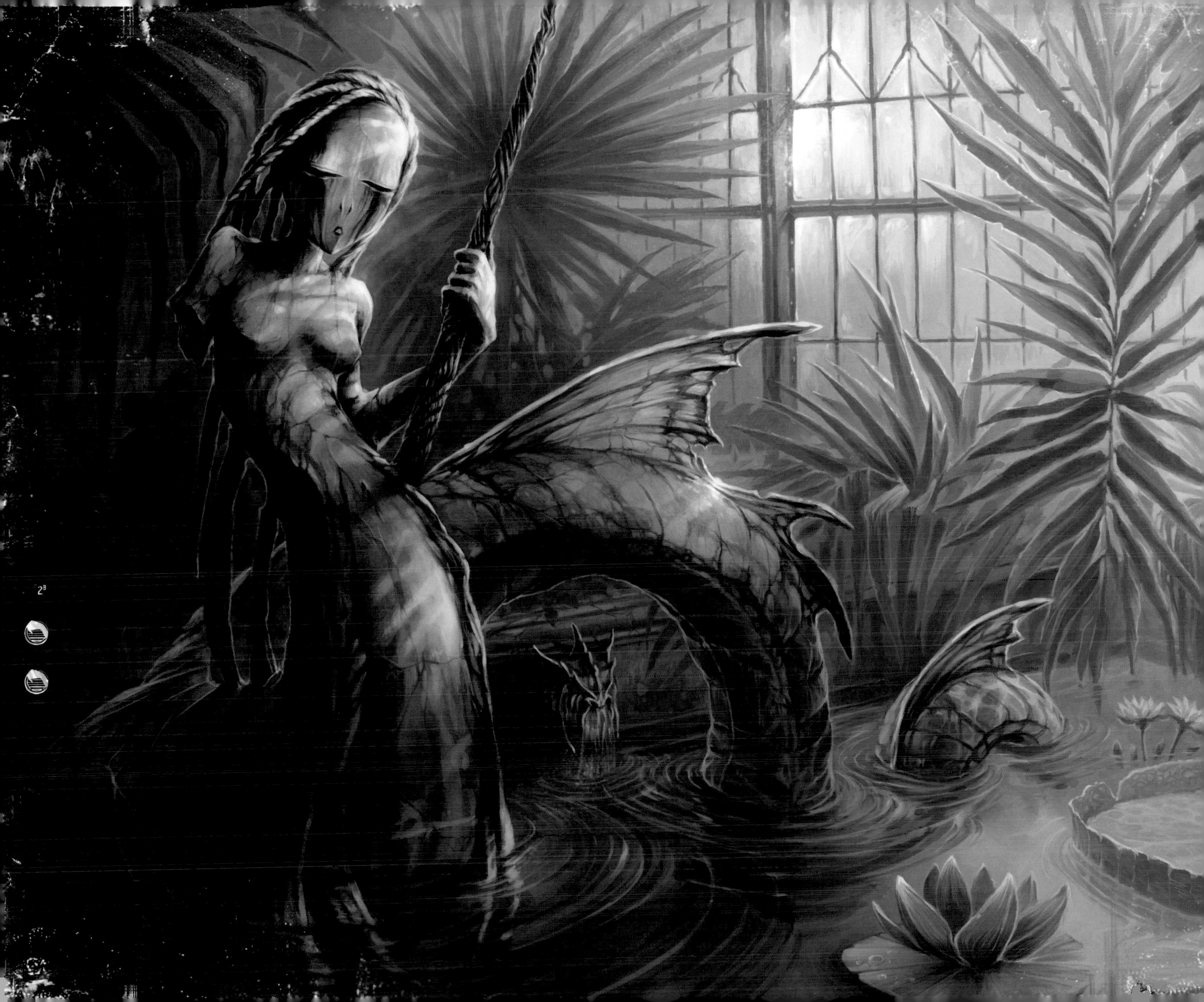

AQUATIC GREENHOUSE

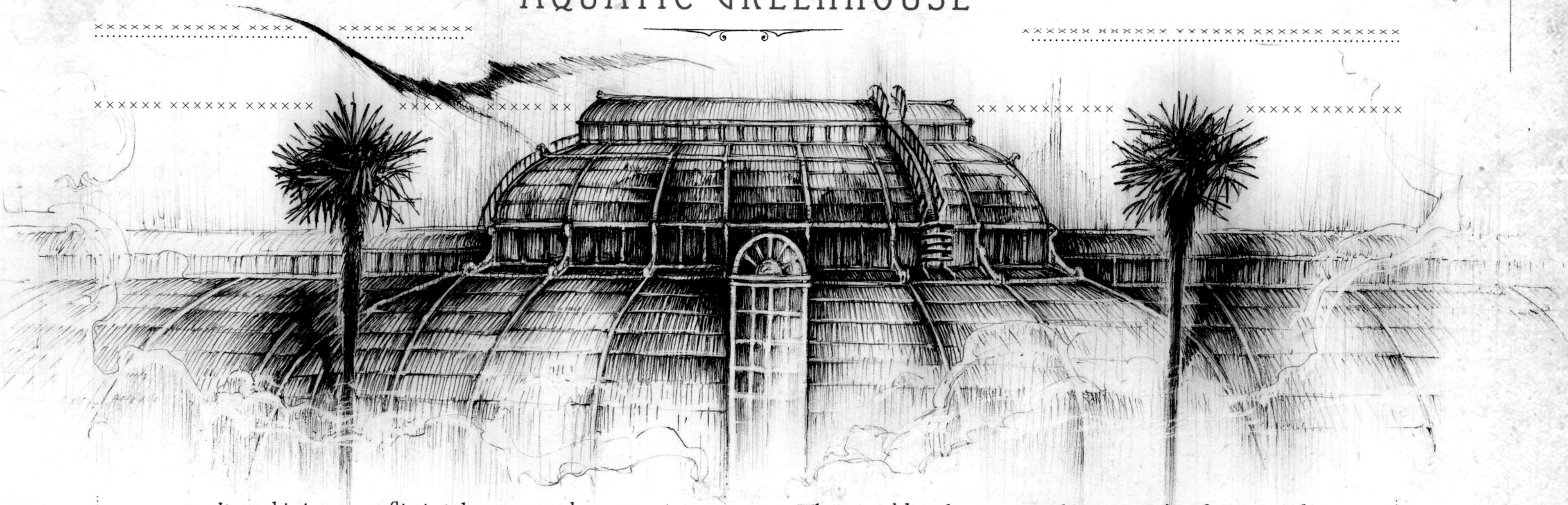

++++++ It was his incessant flitting that attracted my attention. Tapping his beak on the top of the longest of the wooden crates, he managed to make a hollow from which oozed thick black dirt! I was so intrigued I approached and discovered the source of the verdant invasion. It had even taken root inside the crate. Unsettled, I extracted the thing and took it with me so as to better examine it in the Kew Gardens greenhouse. A breath of wind made me realize that the Dragon had followed me. He didn't seem to want to put any distance whatsoever between us! ++++++ In the bright light of the conservatory, I discovered, to my amazement, the intricate design of the coffer. The carvings evoked many pleasant memories!

Where could such a treasure have come from? It seemed so obvious but I didn't want to believe it. After slightly scratching the surface, I discovered a petrified arm, trapped by several roots and I understood! ***This crate was a sarcophagus!*** How could that be and why had the London Park been chosen as a man's final resting place? The answers began to frighten me. ... But they would have to wait, I needed to act, and fast! The wood of the sarcophagus was drying out and turning into dust. ... I needed to soak it.

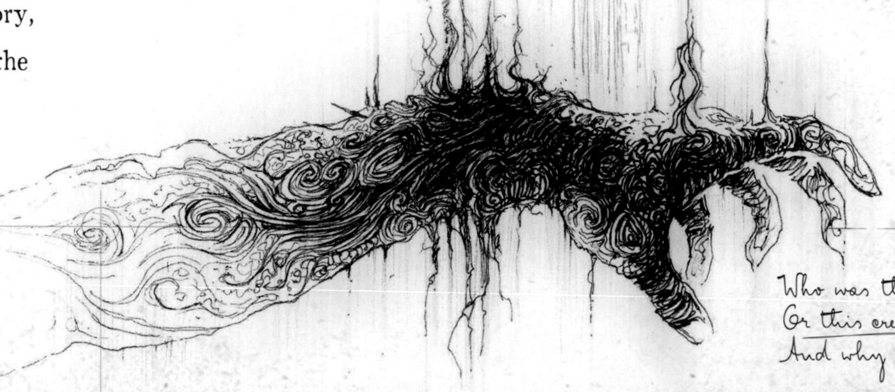

MEMORIES ***FROM THE LAND BEYOND DREAMS*** – *Kew Gardens, the morning of Dec. 29, 1898, 2:00 a.m. GMT*

EXTRACTED MEMORY OF *T. Poppins*

Who was this man?
Or this creature?
And why bring him to me?

Report CLXXX ~ B-2-a

night 01

THE VERDANT SARCOPHAGUS

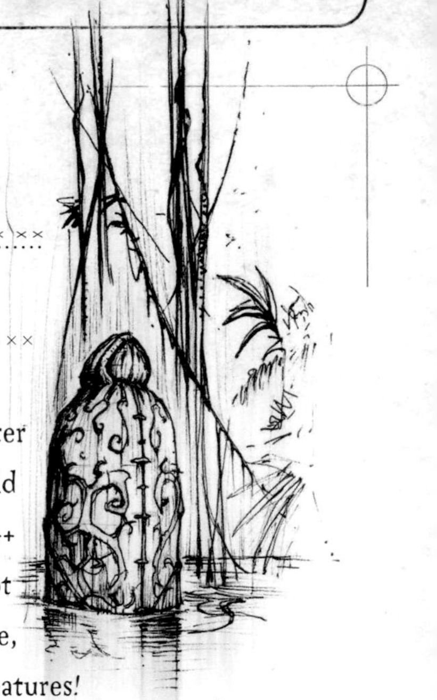

++++++ As though pulled by a final cry for help, the junk's huge frame reached the banks of Kew Gardens. As its bulk approached me, it didn't take me long to recognize its colors. Up on the foremast, the torch on the purple background of the Chimeric Company waved proudly. Where could this ship, considered lost for the last four years, have come from, and what would it reveal? ++++++ Sighing beneath my feet, moaning at the slightest breath of wind that whistled through its rigging, it beckoned me aboard... Though clearly its frame had seen better days, this Titan of the sea was still breathing! I could feel it. There was not a living soul on board. ++++++ O vessel of the Chimeric Company, you cannot — after having sailed so many miles — succumb here, in my Park, for no reason! Empty of all crew or creatures! ++++++ The light of dawn guided my steps — a bit heavy after that flight — around the thick protruding roots that heaved through the deck from the trap to the hold. Though I did what I could to try and clear the knotted greenery, I was not overly delighted to be gardening this early in the morning! Not without difficulty, I managed to get through the ligneous aerophytes and into the bowels of the junk. A jumble of roots and crates floated in muddy water! Two or three birds of paradise greeted me as they escaped. They must have been nesting in this place that had become a jungle long ago! Other than the winged guardian that led me to it, no other creature, mythic or haunted, seemed to dwell within the vessel! A steam-run vehicle languished there, alone, its wheels rooted in the mud! Nonplussed, I wondered if Ma Toshiro hadn't made a mistake, or been duped by her messenger?

Besides, the Bengali's to-ing and fro-ing was making the mandrake go to my head!

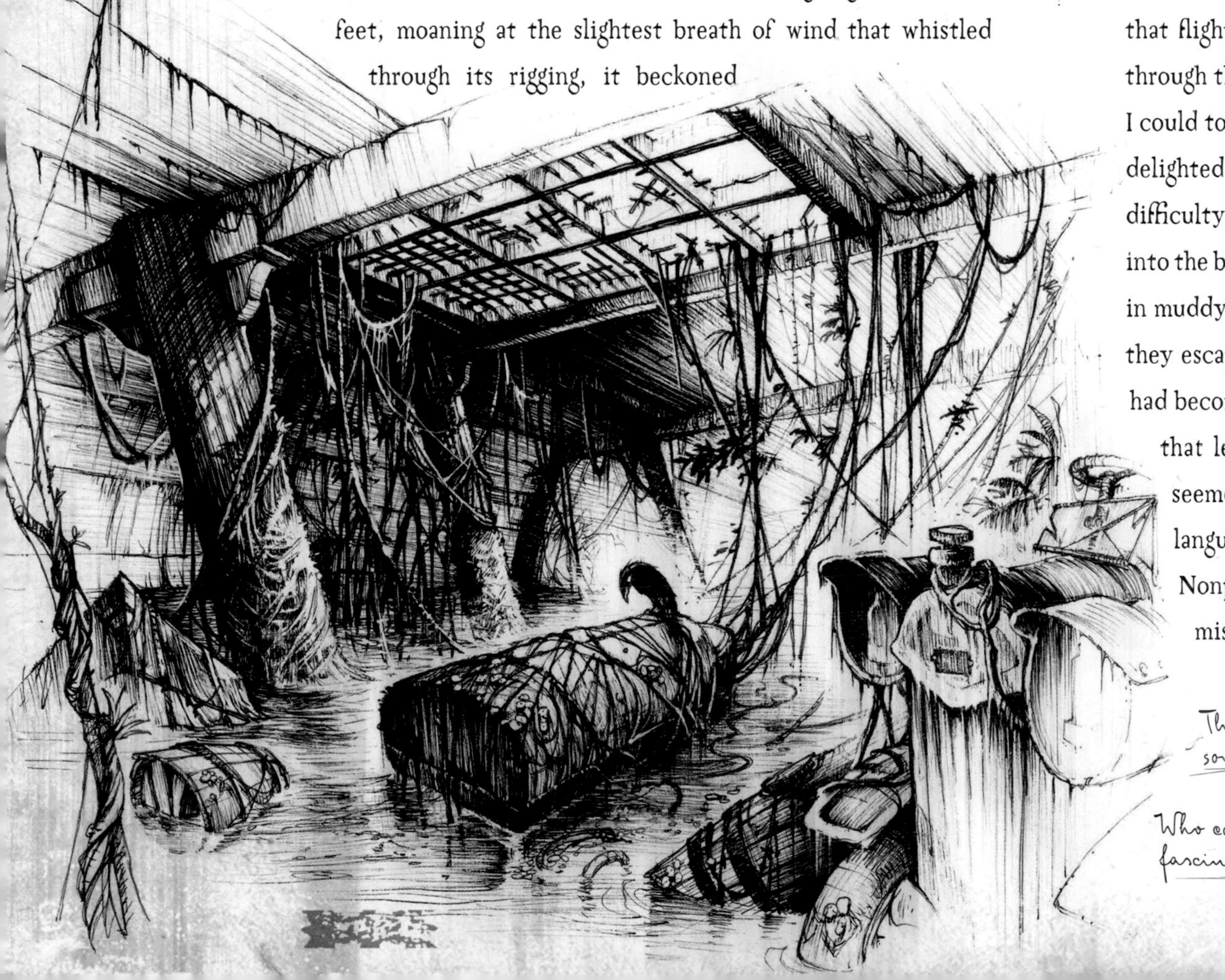

The unusual cargo included someone's automobile.

Who could be the lucky owner of this fascinating little machine?

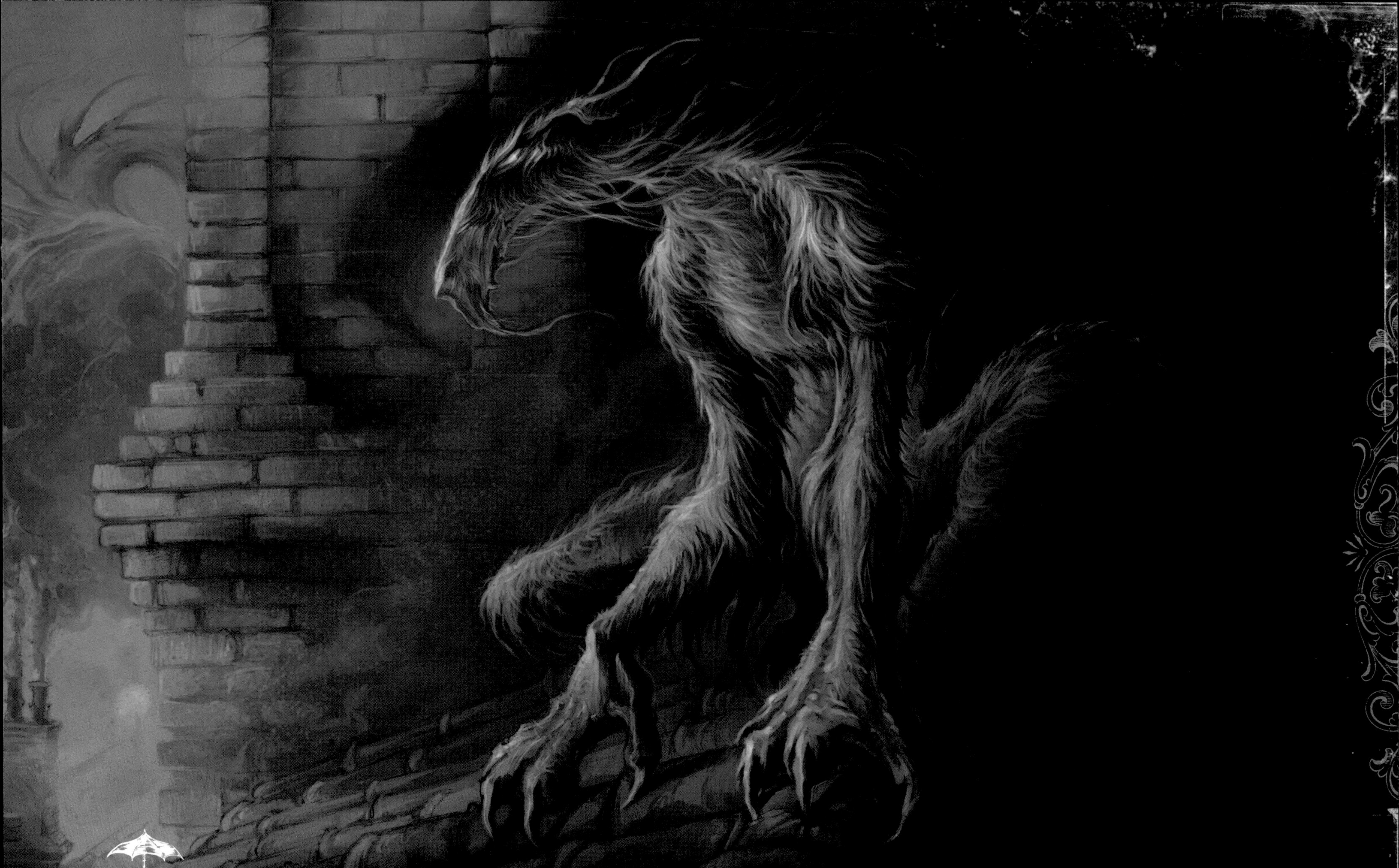

++++++ Personally, I was surprised by Ma Toshiro's claim about the arrival of an ancient creature — but I could not disobey the lady! ~ On her orders, flying by night, I zigzagged above the rooftops and immense chimneys of London. Following that cursed bird, already far ahead of me, was not easy. [...] That feathery circus act of a messenger, showing up as little more than a black arrow in the starless sky, was hard for me to keep up with! Finally... to my great surprise, he headed toward the outskirts of the city. Floundering, I landed in a fog as thick as pea soup, and I have to confess I jumped when a ***wolf man*** brushed past me! The place had already been claimed — I greeted him courteously. Stock still, the animal observed the unfamiliar scene... This creature of shrouded gray mist, a gigantic dragon whose arrival was prophesied, effaced every silhouette as he passed. Enveloped in his fog, almost invisible, a junk, sailing silently, glided toward Kew Gardens. ++++++

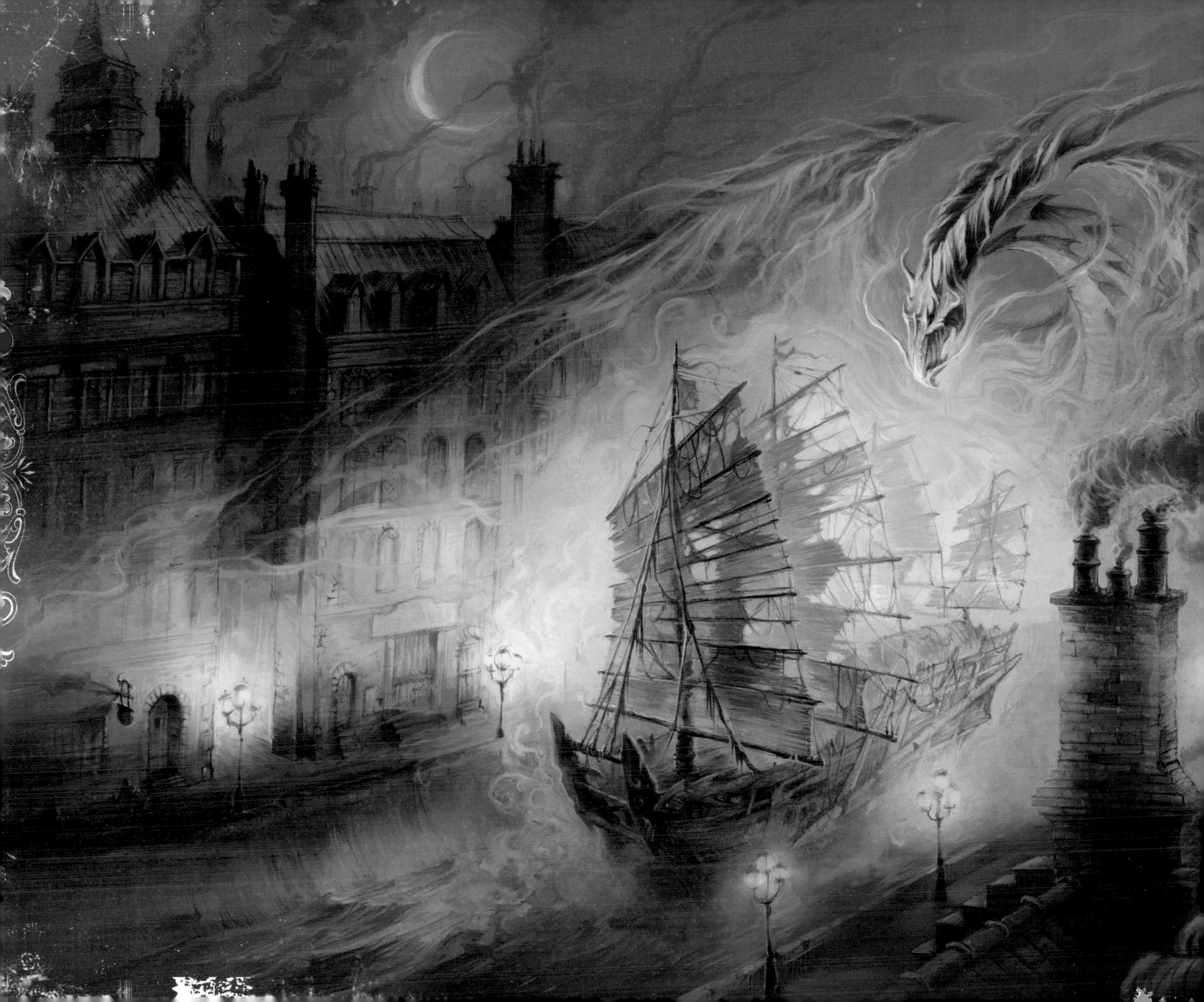

The arrival of AN OLD FRIEND

Report CLXXX ～ B-2-a

45ᵗʰ file

FROM THE YEAR 1898

A SOMBER MESSENGER

14 UMBRELLA 'POPS'

++++++ It's been two years now since the **Chimeric Company** has been ceaselessly amazing Londoners with its flawless performances! Every evening I watch them, almost religiously, as they come out of their tent! [*Ah! The incredible Ma Toshiro! You always knew how to play with your loyal audience's sense of reality! While at the same time making them forget that monocles, hats, and corsets… are not really a must!*] ++++++ The magic of tonight's show was interrupted by the arrival of a dark messenger, a Bengal raven, who flew across the stage to land on the (little) lady's hand. An experienced falconer, she attached the corvid's talons to her leather glove. Together they made a deadly pair. During their entire long collusion, they did not exchange a word. Only the two dragons tattooed face to face on her chin quivered… She'd gone pale, and with a look, she invited me to follow her backstage.
"Warden, something serious is afoot. My deity the raven just informed me that a powerful creature is approaching. +++ Give him the welcome he deserves, Sir Theodore Jolicœur Poppins!" +++++++ As she spoke those words, the raven flew off, knocking me unconscious with his great wing as he passed.

Slightly shaken, the falconer went back to her favorite pastime, and I'm pretty sure, some of her own product!

R

2

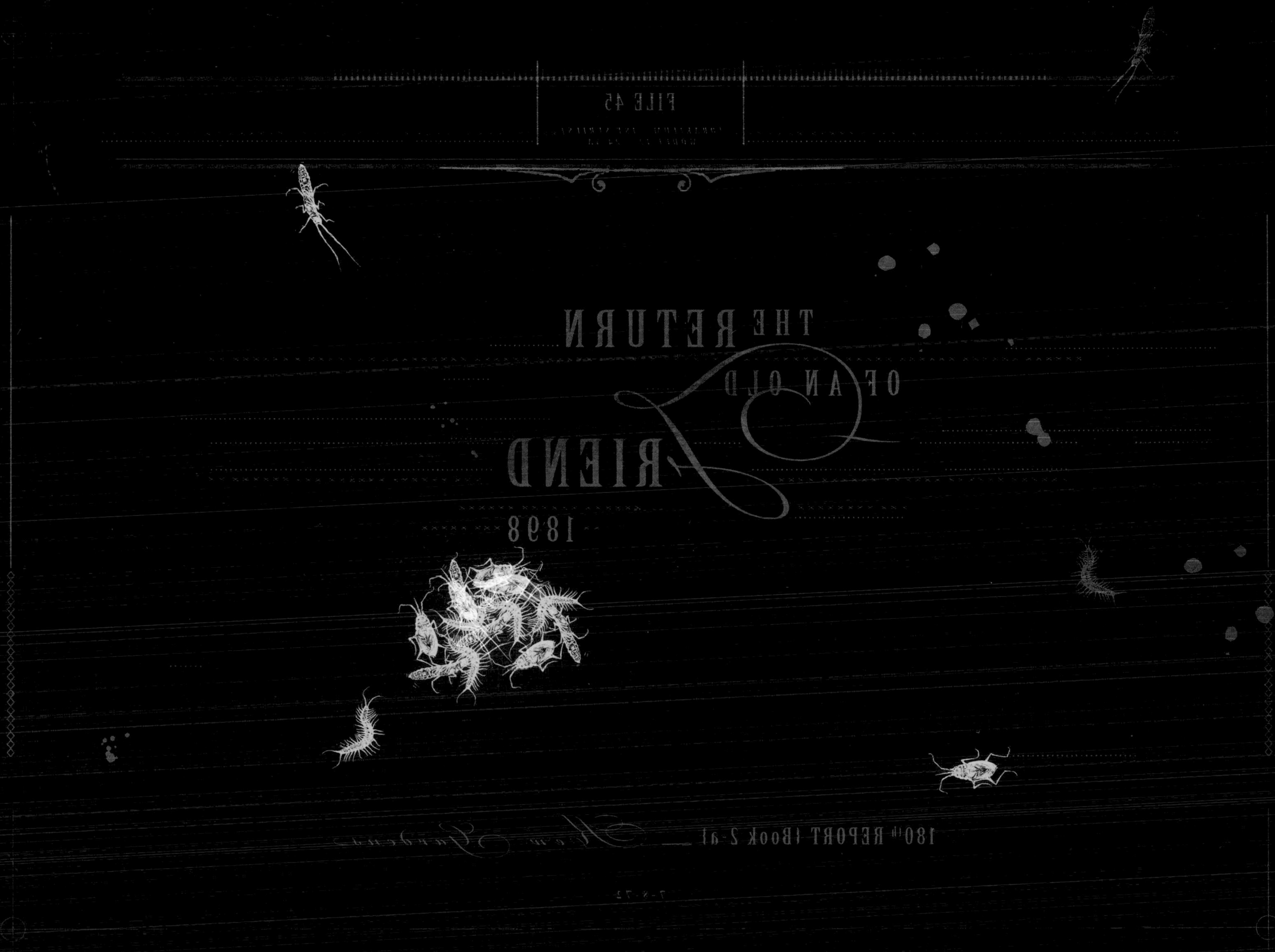
FILE 45
THE RETURN OF AN OLD FRIEND
1898
180th REPORT (Book 2-a)

x xxxxxx x *—Kensington Gardens, evening of Dec. 28, 1898, 8:15 p.m. GMT* - MEMORY OUTPUT ANOMALY VIA *Orakilum*

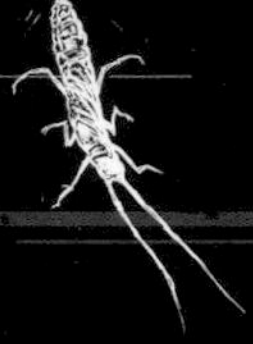

45TH FILE

[ORAKILUM : 1ST SERIES]
MODEL 12 - 24.5A

THE RETURN OF AN OLD FRIEND

1898

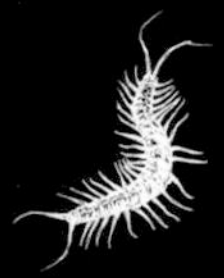

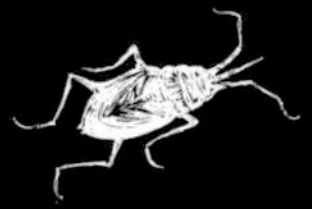

180th REPORT {Book 2-a} — Kew Gardens

8-7-72

THE GREAT ANGUILLA, SEPT. 14, 1896, 2:00 A.M. GMT

2^B

IIIIOII III

XXXXX XXXXXX XXXXX XXXXXX XXXXXX

SPECTRAL MERMAID. —*Kensington Gardens,*

CITY ARCHIVE IMAGE VIA *Orakilum*

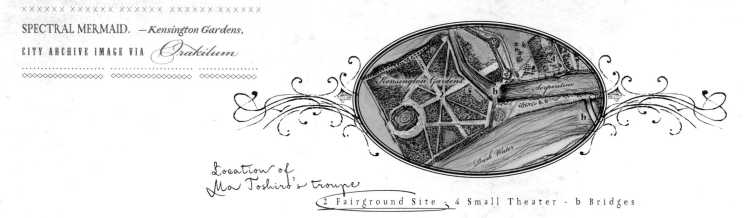

Location of
Ma Toshiro's troupe

2 Fairground Site - 4 Small Theater - b Bridges

++++++ My friends, to wrap up this masquerade, a final act will be added tonight. The dream weaver will once more fill their heads right here in the heart of London. They are going to be captivated by an incredible closing chorale, one that our stilt walker refers to as the " *velvety voiced finale* "!

O magnificent *Siren,*
(beautiful specter)
your song of sorrow will quash the melancholy secret that you have carried with you since Prague... Lost soul of the dark waters, Scheherazade of those eternal thousand and one nights, you will amaze them in revealing your true being, your immortality, which will conceal the Goliaths' entrance. Cradled by your enchanting voice, put to sleep by the performance, the spectators will never know who we took in this evening. It's a perfect plan, I can assure you of that! ++++++

++++++ *Golem, lost child of Prague, dream in peace, there under the dead Tree. Fear not, the Park of the Chimeras will always be there to protect you.*

END OF THE REPORT ON THE ARRIVAL OF THE PROTECTORS.

—KENSINGTON GARDENS +++++

GOLEM, SEPT. 15, 1896 - 11 P.M. GMT.

Theodore P.

CONFIDENTIAL

2

4444444444444

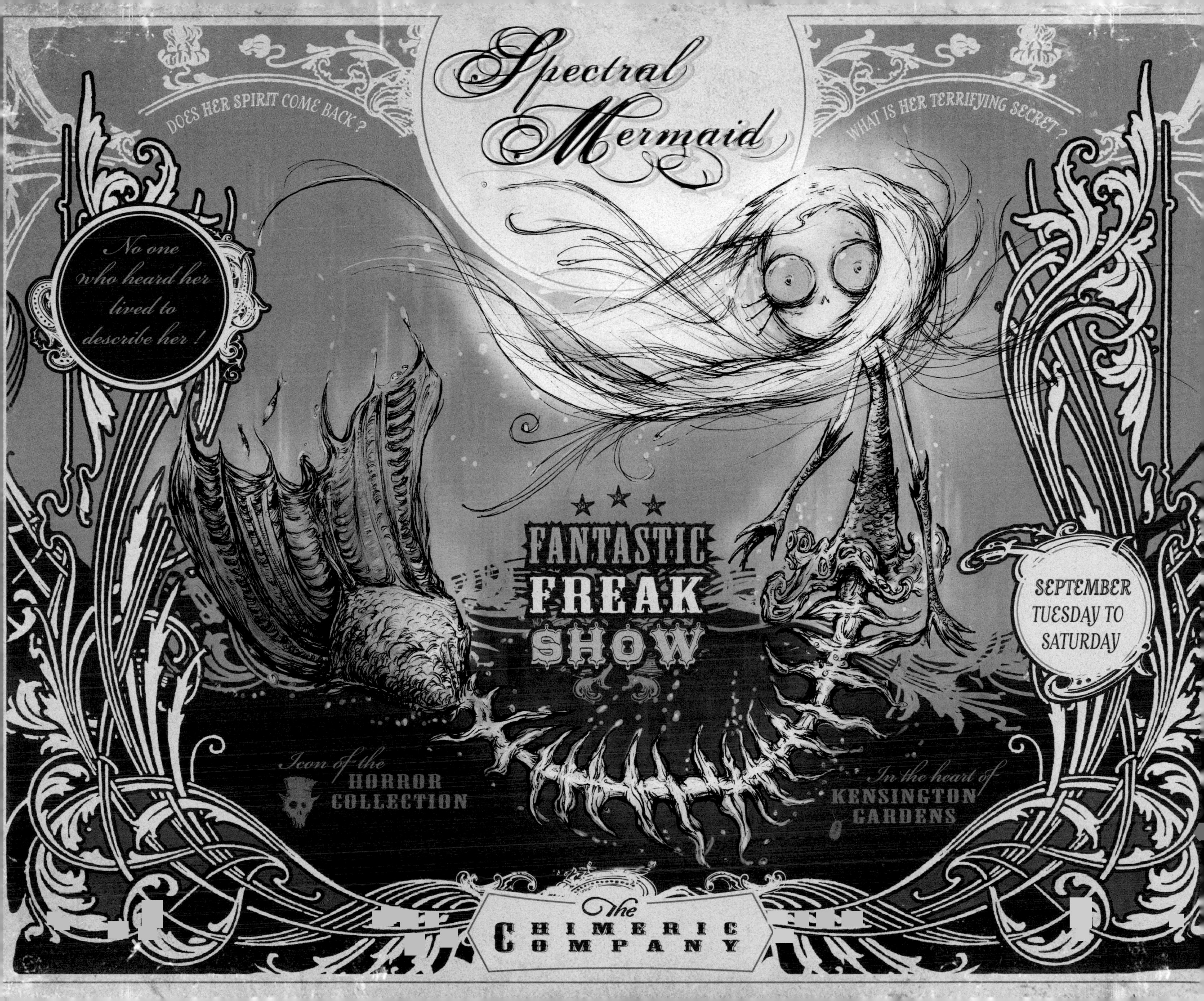
Spectral Mermaid
DOES HER SPIRIT COME BACK ?
WHAT IS HER TERRIFYING SECRET ?
No one who heard her lived to describe her !
FANTASTIC
FREAK
SHOW
SEPTEMBER
TUESDAY TO
SATURDAY
Icon of the
HORROR
COLLECTION
In the heart of
KENSINGTON
GARDENS
The
CHIMERIC
COMPANY

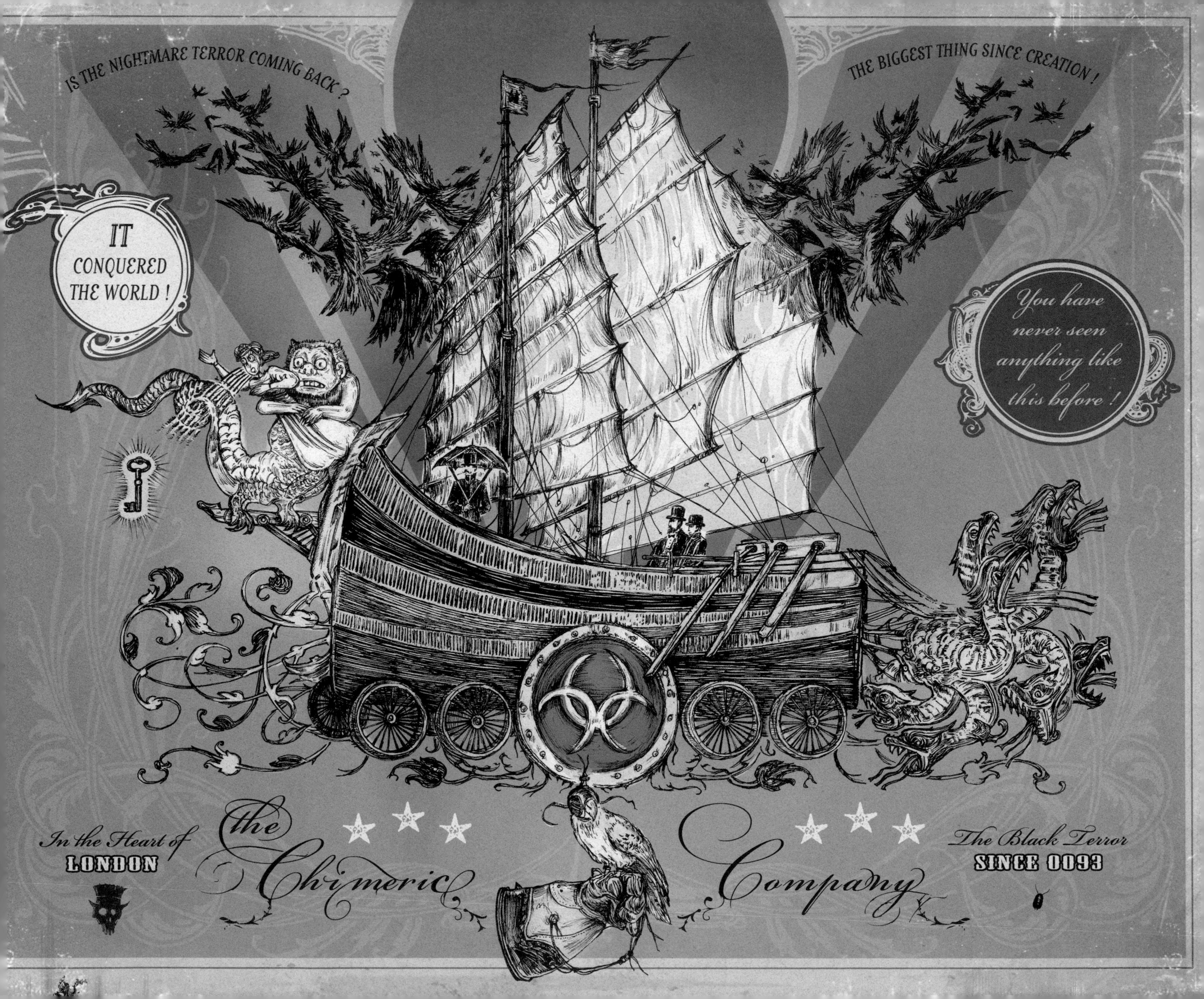
IS THE NIGHTMARE TERROR COMING BACK ?
THE BIGGEST THING SINCE CREATION !
IT CONQUERED THE WORLD !
You have never seen anything like this before !
In the Heart of LONDON
the Chimeric Company
The Black Terror SINCE 0093

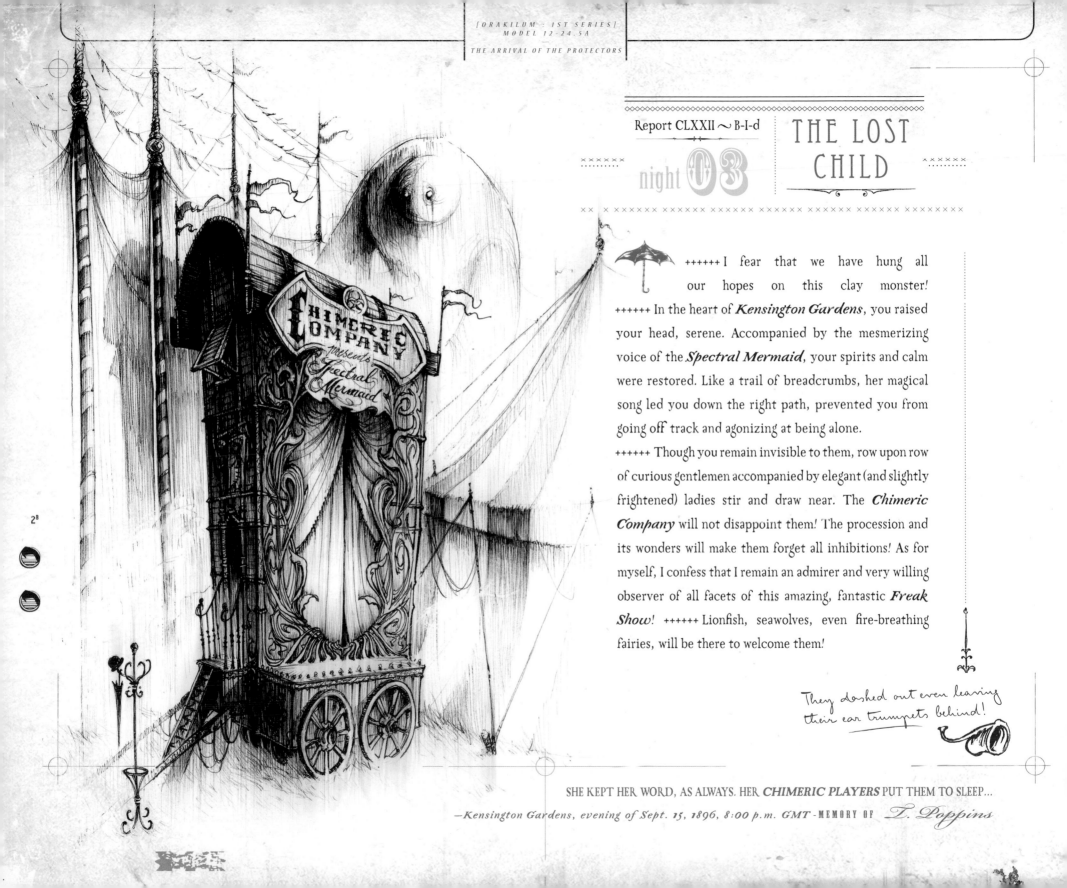

Report CLXXII ~ B-I-d

night 03

THE LOST CHILD

++++++ I fear that we have hung all our hopes on this clay monster!

++++++ In the heart of ***Kensington Gardens***, you raised your head, serene. Accompanied by the mesmerizing voice of the ***Spectral Mermaid***, your spirits and calm were restored. Like a trail of breadcrumbs, her magical song led you down the right path, prevented you from going off track and agonizing at being alone.

++++++ Though you remain invisible to them, row upon row of curious gentlemen accompanied by elegant (and slightly frightened) ladies stir and draw near. The ***Chimeric Company*** will not disappoint them! The procession and its wonders will make them forget all inhibitions! As for myself, I confess that I remain an admirer and very willing observer of all facets of this amazing, fantastic ***Freak Show***! ++++++ Lionfish, seawolves, even fire-breathing fairies, will be there to welcome them!

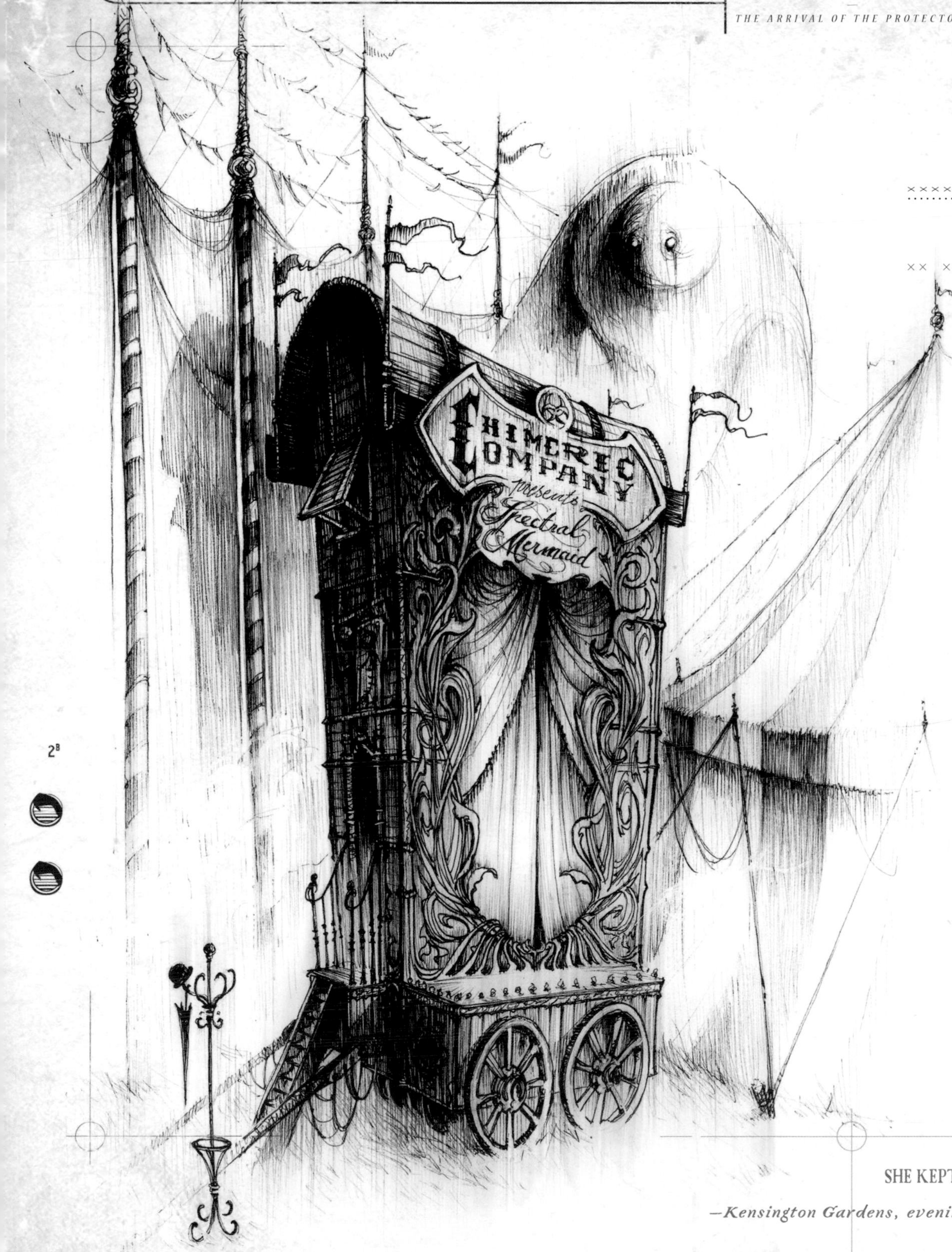
Chimeric Company
presents
Spectral Mermaid

2B

They dashed out even leaving their ear trumpets behind!

SHE KEPT HER WORD, AS ALWAYS. HER ***CHIMERIC PLAYERS*** PUT THEM TO SLEEP...

—Kensington Gardens, evening of Sept. 15, 1896, 8:00 p.m. GMT - MEMORY OF *T. Poppins*

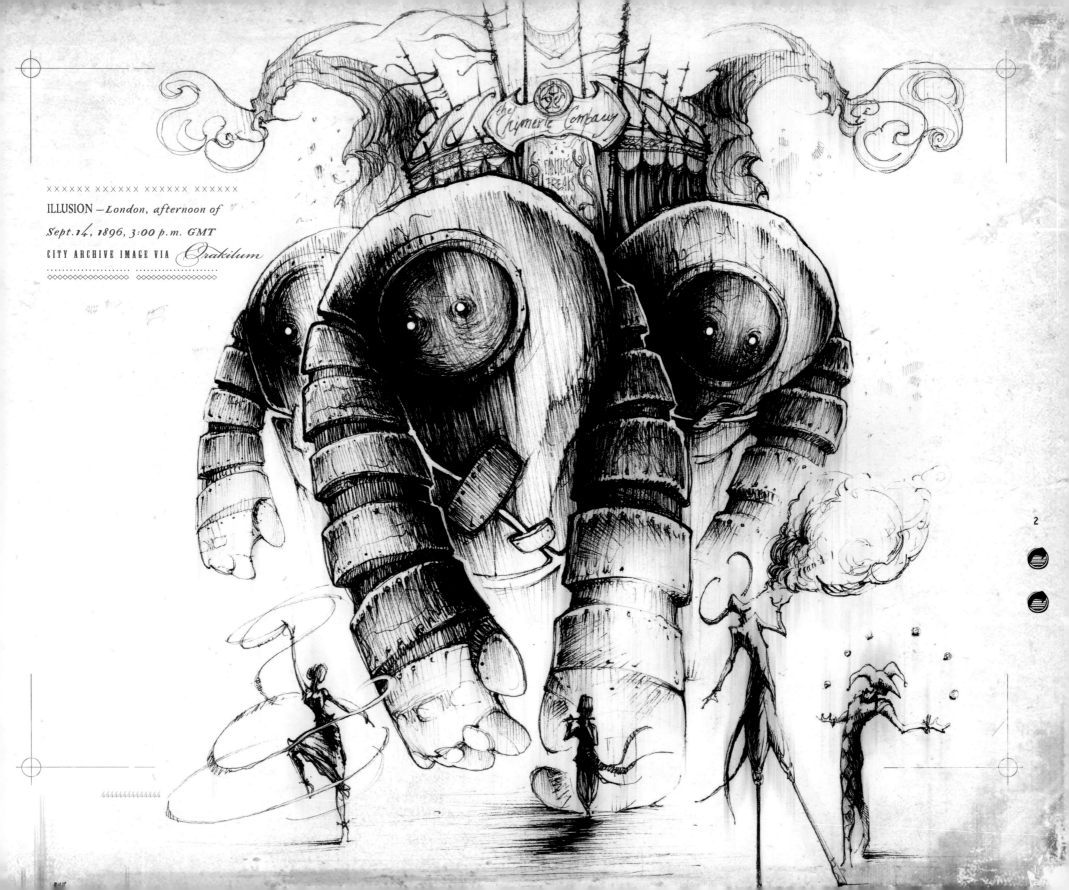

ILLUSION —*London, afternoon of Sept. 14, 1896, 3:00 p.m. GMT*
CITY ARCHIVE IMAGE VIA *Orakilum*

Report CLXXII ~ B-1-d

day 02

THE CHIMERIC COMPANY

++++++ It was broad daylight when the amazing procession appeared in the London streets! Frosty as ever, Ma Toshiro led her troupe proudly. Her fantastic band of players flowed slowly and languidly through the narrow alleyways of the East End. She knew how to capture her audience, and no one noticed the strange mood in the midst of this bacchanalian hullabaloo.

++++++ *"Children of London, come and listen! Discover the most incredible and fantastic mysteries ever revealed since the dawn of time! Before your very eyes, the never-before-seen, mysterious, unique Chimeric Company will pitch its tent — for an unspecified period of time and only a stone's throw from your homes, in the heart of Kensington Gardens.* ++++++ ++++++ ++++++ *Let yourself get swept away into nights of sheer terror by hydras and phantoms! Every evening at twilight, our creatures will be most honoured to perform for you, dear London friends..."* ++++++

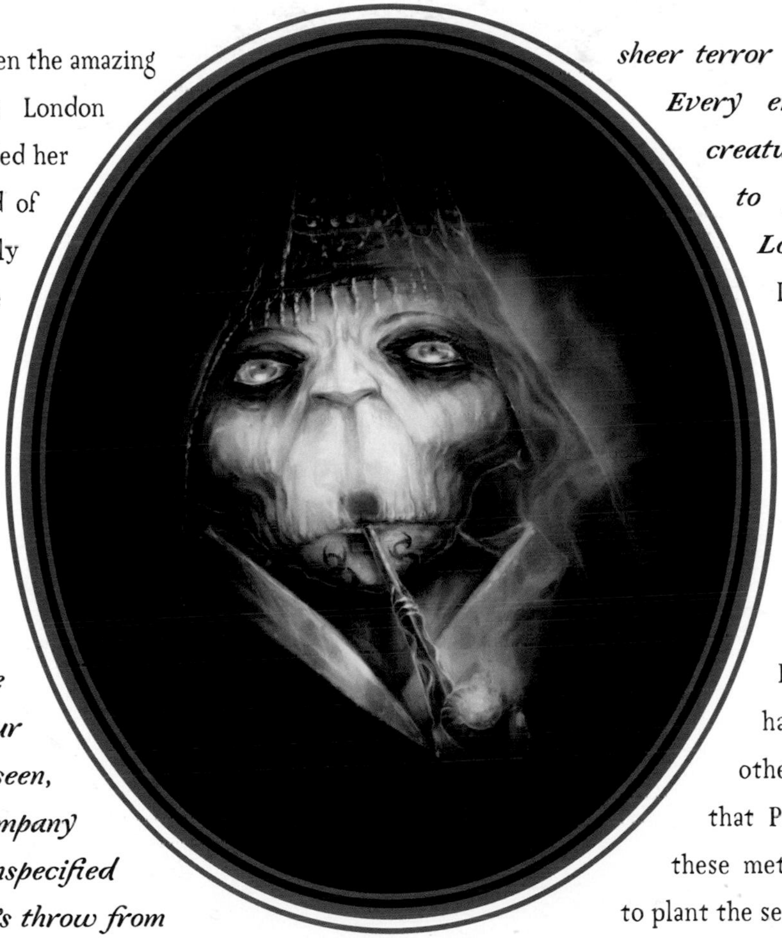

I smiled as I listened to my old acquaintance shout. ++++++

[This tactic seemed to have worked, distracting the bystanders.] +++++++++

Before, I would have found this ploy far too dangerous, but the lost child of Rabbi Loew, this ***Golem***, could not have been lured to the Park any other way. Drawn by the sound of that Pied Piper, these automatons, these metallic monsters, had managed to plant the seeds of doubt and confusion in the hunters' minds. +++++ This charade had created the illusion necessary to ensure survival.

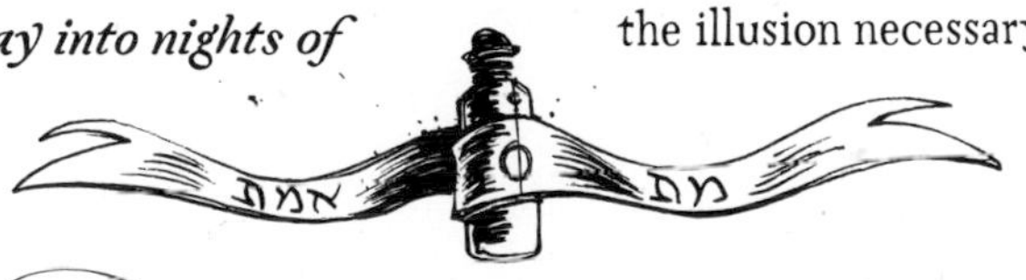
אמת
מת

Their Formula Vitae is in good hands.
Ma Toshiro can be quite terrifying.

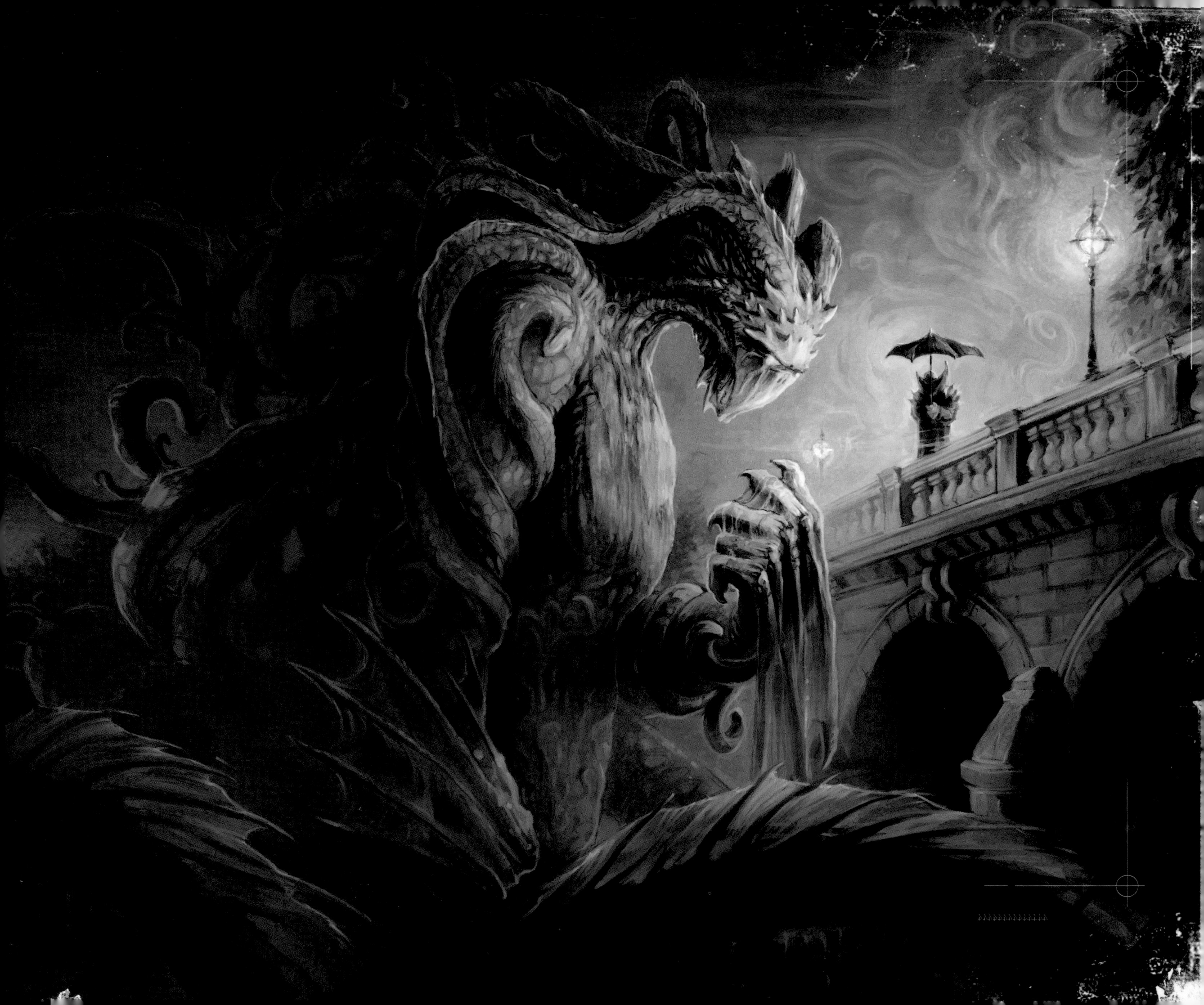

Report CLXXII~B-I-d

night 01

THE SECRET OF THE WATERS OF THE THAMES

++++++ After having crossed the bridge over the Serpentine for the umpteenth time, I started to worry. I was certain that he would come, though, so I decided to wait a little longer... Had I dozed off? ++++++ *[Maybe.]* ++++++ When I lifted my head, startled by a quiet bubbling, many long hours had passed. I leant over the railing and through the darkness I could make out the enchanted waters. He finally awoke, but the surface of the river stayed unbroken, following his lead. Then, rearing out of the water, the ***Great Anguilla*** looked at me. I saw the lights of the city dancing in his black eyes. His slithering body, made up of teeming leptocephali, came alive when he spoke. It was important that I understood him straightaway, and although his Sabir was not good, I was pleased to learn that no other deplorable incident had taken place in the heart of London. The Guild was being oddly discreet. They were trying to provoke me — that was certain! But the arrival of Ma Toshiro's troupe at the docks of the East End would keep us one step ahead. ++++++ I looked on as the creature unraveled into a multitude of eels that wove in and out of each other and disappeared to the bottom through the kelp.

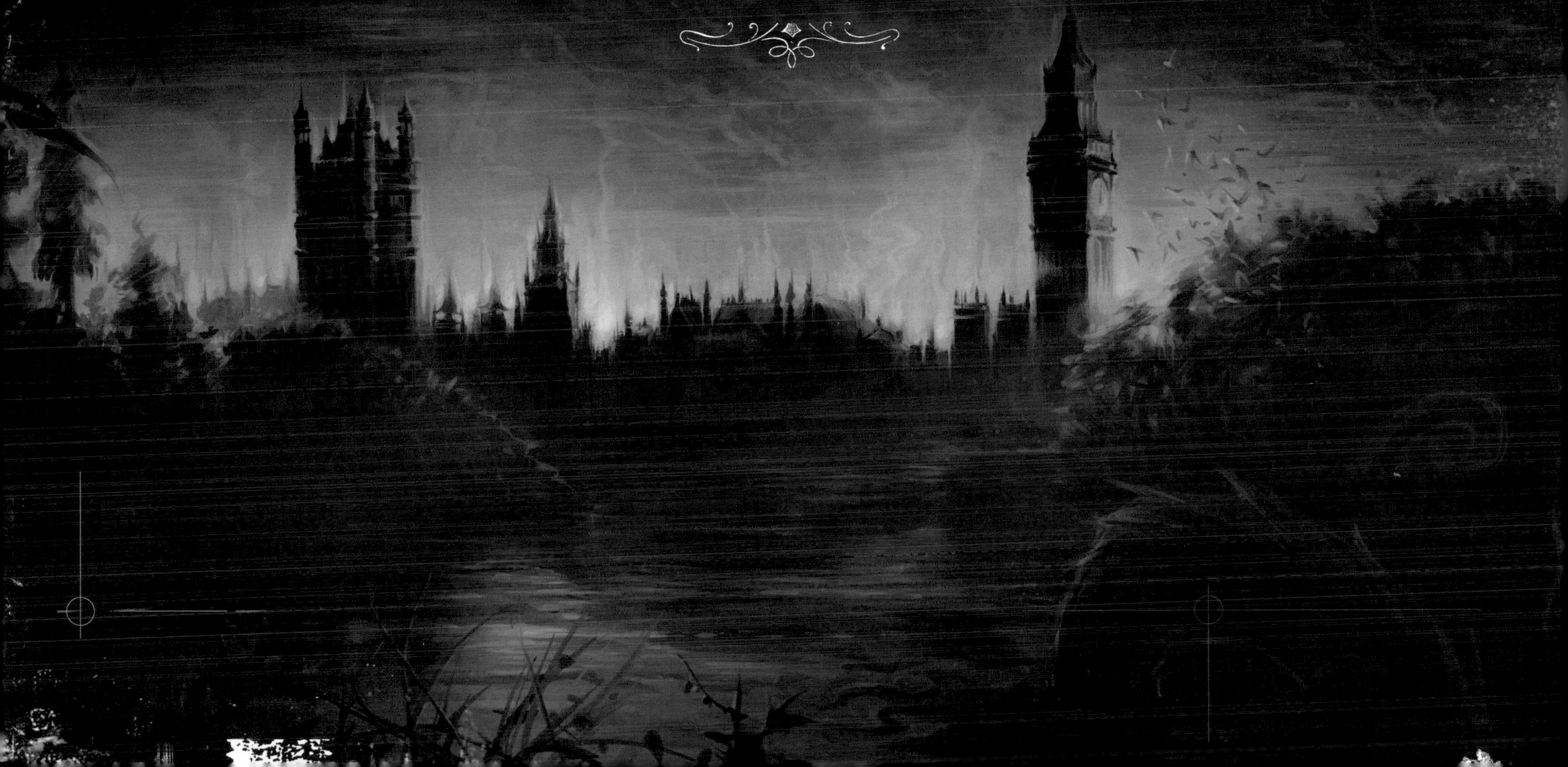

The arrival of THE PROTECTORS

Report CLXXII ~ B-I-d

43RD file

FROM THE YEAR 1896

THEIR
CALLING CARD

09 UMBRELLA 'POPS'

BET ON THE ACE OF
SPADES NEXT TIME!

++++++ *An ace of spades* at Decimus's house, how could they have done that? Rob his old home on Dock Street, while he rests in peace at the Kensal Green Cemetery, dead these fifteen years. ~~Vandals!~~ *Barbarians* !!! It bears all the hallmarks of *the Harquebusier of the East End!* By now, several of his cards must have been tossed about.++++++ *[My steps resonated in the empty living room; my brain was suddenly empty.]* ++++++ ++++++ ++++++ ++++++ This unlucky event restarted the game and once again their shadow hangs over the Park! ++++++ *The incident of October 10, 1874,* seems to have been just the beginning of their strategy for launching a new hunt that they could carry out openly! Breaking into Decimus's house could not have given them any clues — the roots still covered the breach. I am still worried about the London Guild's projects and must get back to the banks of the Serpentine to learn more. Someone is expecting me.

++++++ ++++++ ++++++

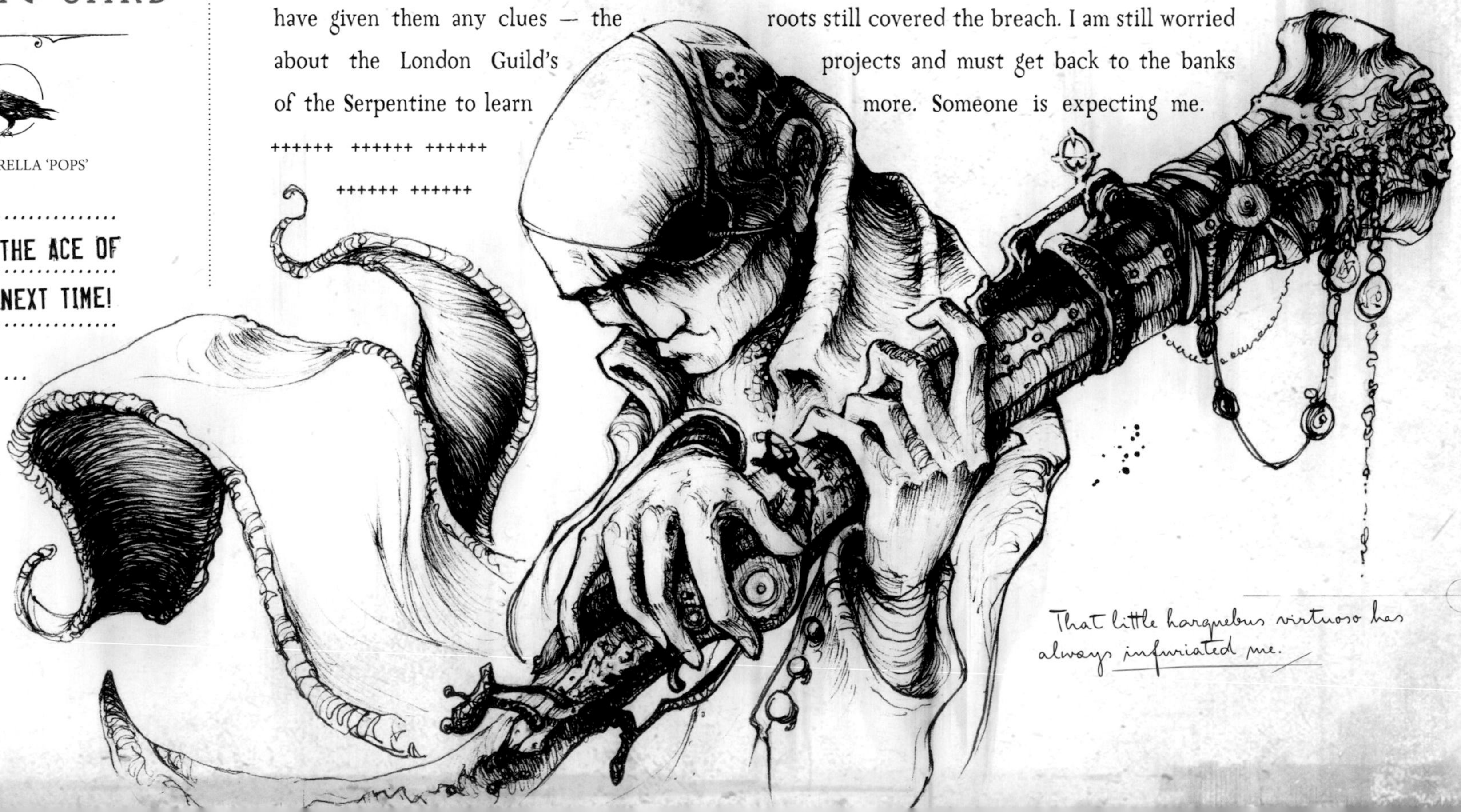

++++++ ++++++

That little harquebus virtuoso has always infuriated me.

2

A

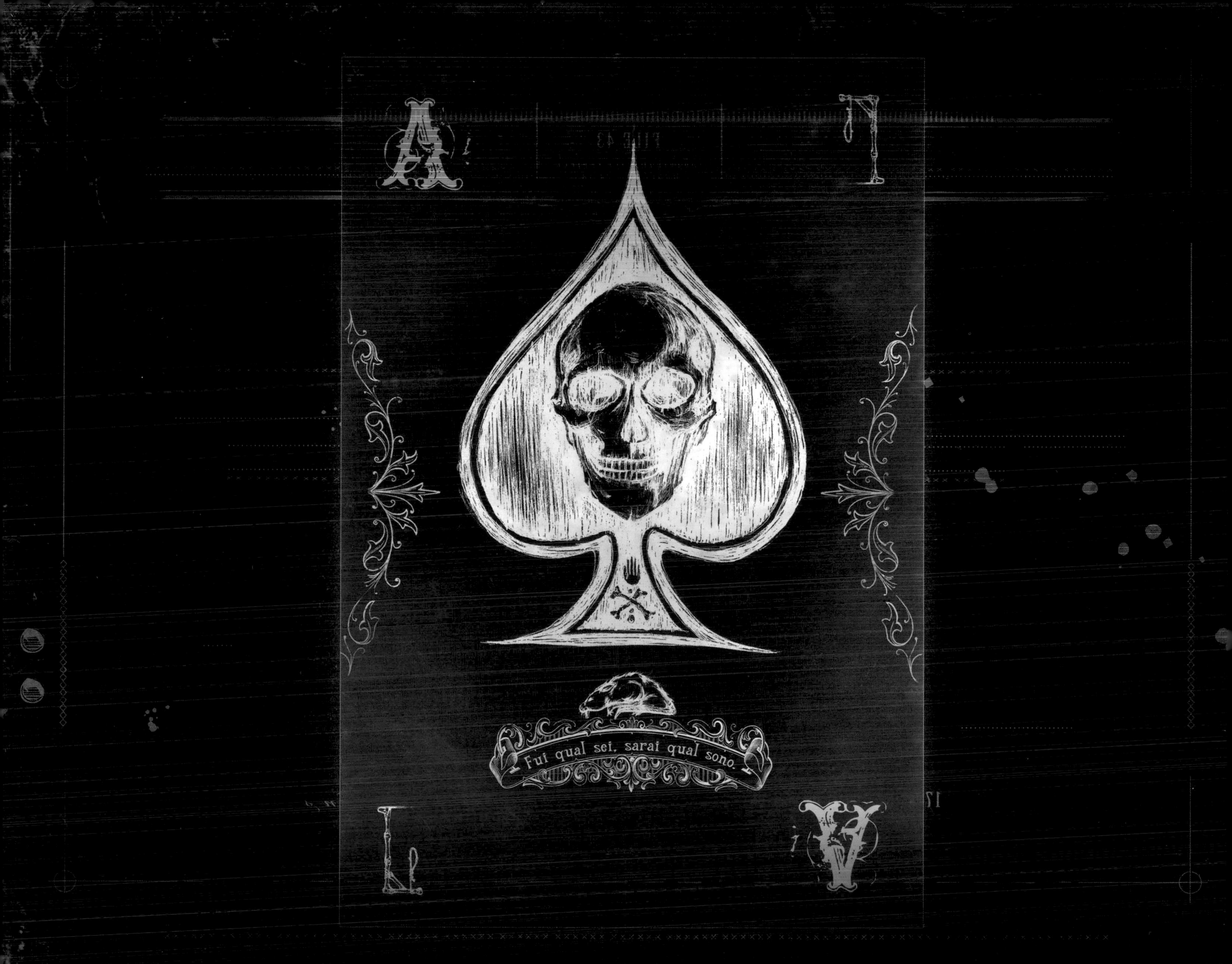
Fui qual sei, sarai qual sono.

XXXXX —*Dock street, evening of Sept. 13, 1896, 11:00 p.m. GMT* - CITY ARCHIVE IMAGE VIA *Orakilum*

43RD FILE

[ORAKILUM : 1ST SERIES]
MODEL 12 - 24.5A

THE ARRIVAL OF THE PROTECTORS 1896

4

172nd REPORT {book 1 - d} _ Kensington Gardens

8-7-72

THE SILVANUS, OCT. 15, 1874 · 6:00 A.M. GMT

IIIIOII III

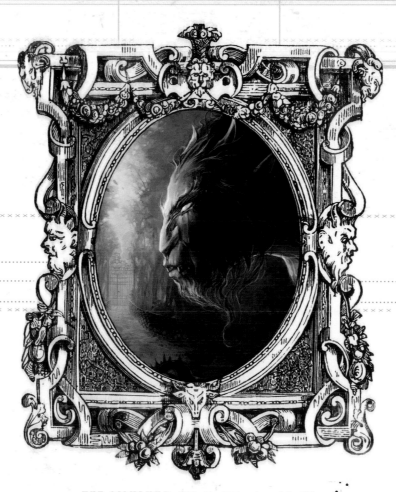

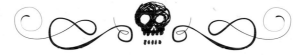

XXXXXX XXXXXX XXXXXX XXXXXX XXXXXX XXXXXX

Between ***MIST*** and ***FOG***.

—Regent's Park, morning of Oct. 16, 1874, 8:00 a.m. GMT

CITY ARCHIVE IMAGE VIA *Orakilum*

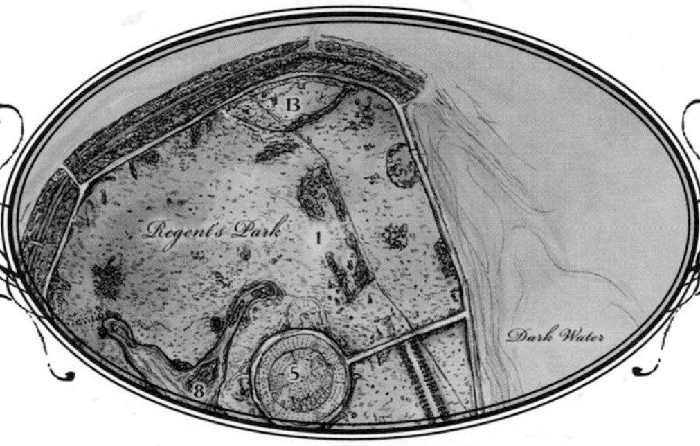
Regent's Park
1
5
8
13
Dark Water

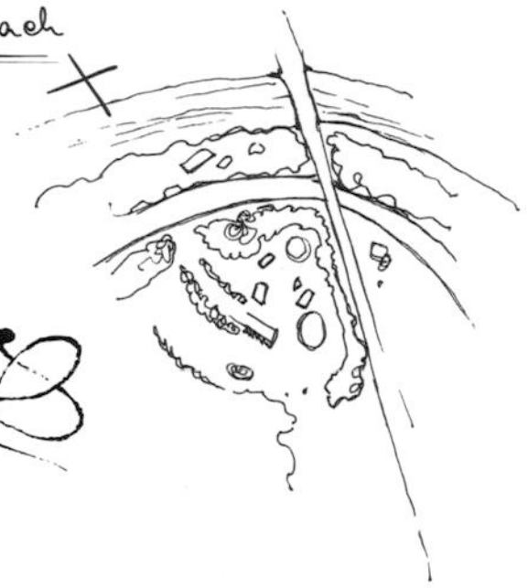
impact of the breach

1 Rose Garden - 5 Chimera Greenhouse - 8 Infirmary - 13 Zoo

++++++ As I am finishing your report, I already see the *fog* coming in. As is its wont, it will manage to seep into the memory of Londoners, so that by early morning not even a trace of past events will linger to haunt them. ++++++

++++++ By the time the first visitors are taking their Sunday constitutionals amid the park's labyrinth of pathways, our dear gardener's ***Drosera rotundifolia*** will have been fully interwoven with the magnificent roots of the indigenous plants. ++++++ ++++++ ++++++ ++++++ ++++++

The strollers will once again be safe in their thoughts, far from lingering horrors. That's the magic of London's parks, and this first ***Garden of Shadows***.

++++++ We already know that in a few years, very little of this incident will remain other than: ***"On October 10, 1874, a barge filled with gunpowder blew out the fences of the Regent's Park zoo."***

END OF REPORT ON THE INCIDENT OF OCTOBER 10, 1874.

—REGENT'S PARK ++++++

THE BREACH, OCT. 16, 1874 · 3 AM · GMT

Theodore P.

CLASSIFIED

You can reach me at the usual address!

2

4444444444444

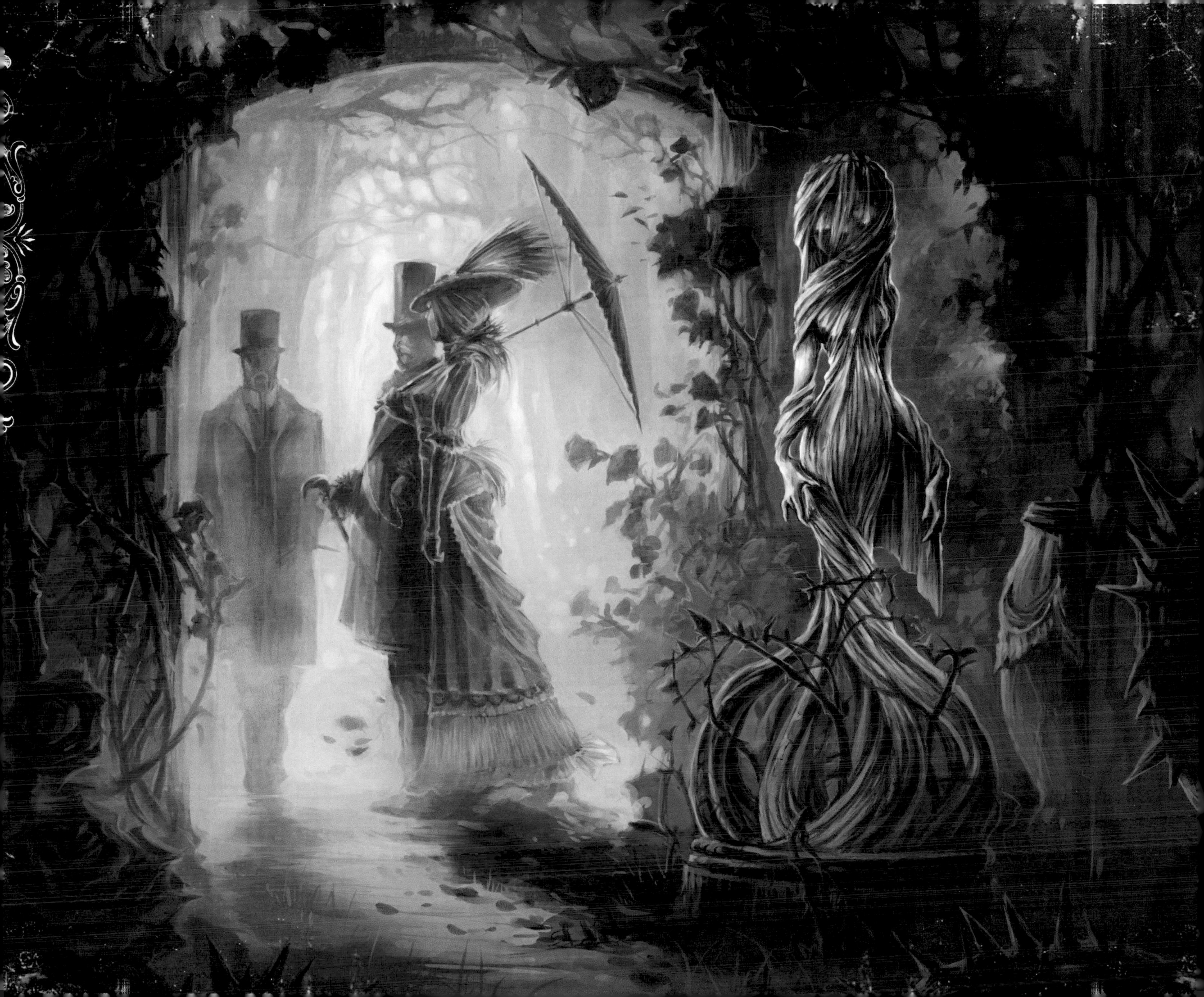

Report CII ~ B-I-b

night 06

DECIMUS BURTON

The gardener's <u>talents</u> never did much for me!

When he arrived, I didn't need to say anything. Our <u>fears were one and the same.</u> He said to me:

— That's not possible! Such an explosion should never have caused that much damage. I'm very sorry, my dear Theodore. ++++++ ++++++ ++++++ ++++++ ++++++

— Decimus, why can't you just redesign the northern fence right now?

He smiled and explained.

— My friend, I dreamt up this ancient place to be immune to all danger. Let's not forget its architecture is not only made up of dead organic matter, grills, and bolts... meaning a whole range of plant life is at your disposal! ++++++ ++++++ ++++++ ++++++ ++++++ ++++++

— The gardener, are you sure ? ++++++

— Quite sure. The time has come. ++++++ ++++++

++++++I acquiesced. Much as I disliked awakening Radix Dormitor, I had no other choice. ++++++ ++++++ ++++++ ++++++

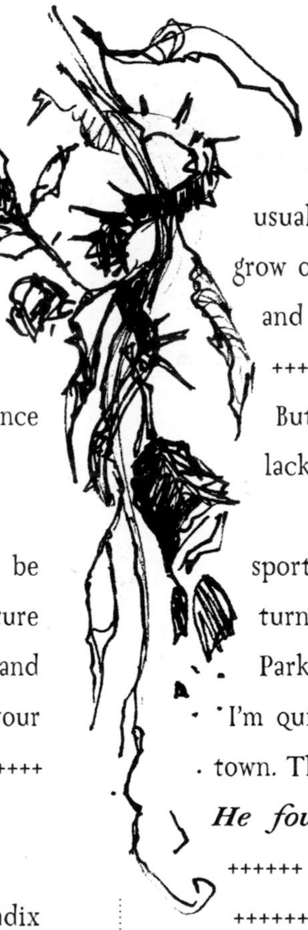

++++++ He responded to my call straightaway and, as usual, the results were instantaneous. Roots started to grow out of the pathways, slowly obeying him. Squealing and moaning, they headed toward the breach, sealing it. ++++++ ++++++ ++++++

But as I had feared, this "artist" used a medium that lacked precision and tended to be a tad invasive!

The inevitable happened. The brambles made sport of everything, even of us! Before we had time to turn and look, they had already <u>covered up all of Regent's</u> Park's fences. If I hadn't asked him to stop it at once, I'm quite certain that he would have covered the whole town. That wouldn't have bothered him in the least, he said. ***He found the idea rather appealing!*** ++++++

2

every seed that had ever been planted in the Park was <u>under his aegis</u>.

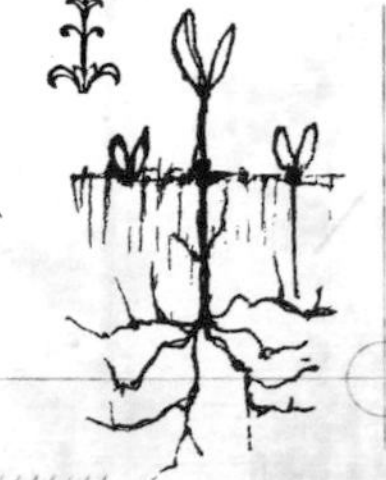

The Bramble Tamer (Radix Dormitor): his dream ~ entangling our world with vegetation. —*Regent's Park, evening of Oct. 15, 1874, 11:30 p.m. GMT*

EXTRACTED MEMORY OF *T. Poppins*

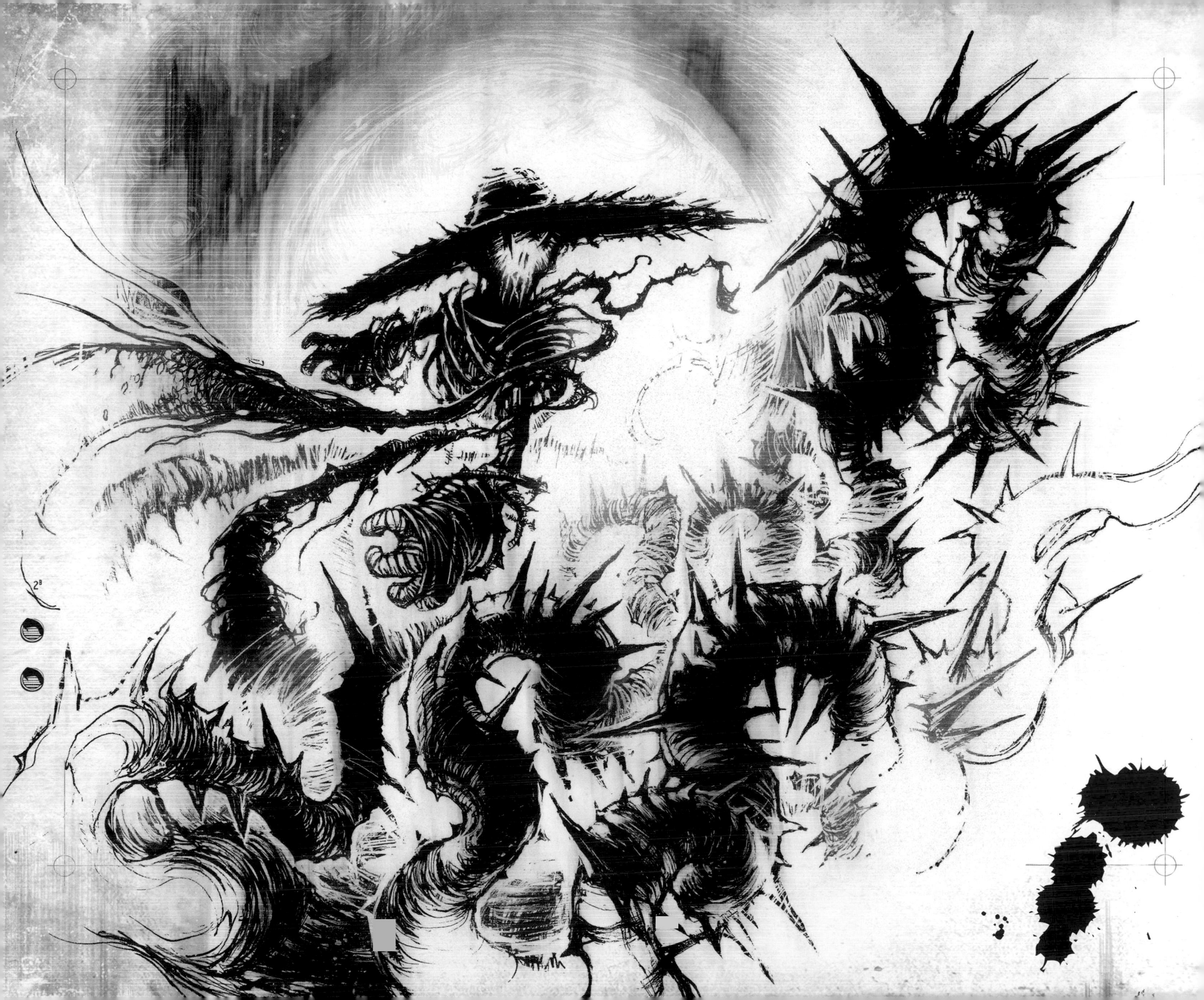
2B

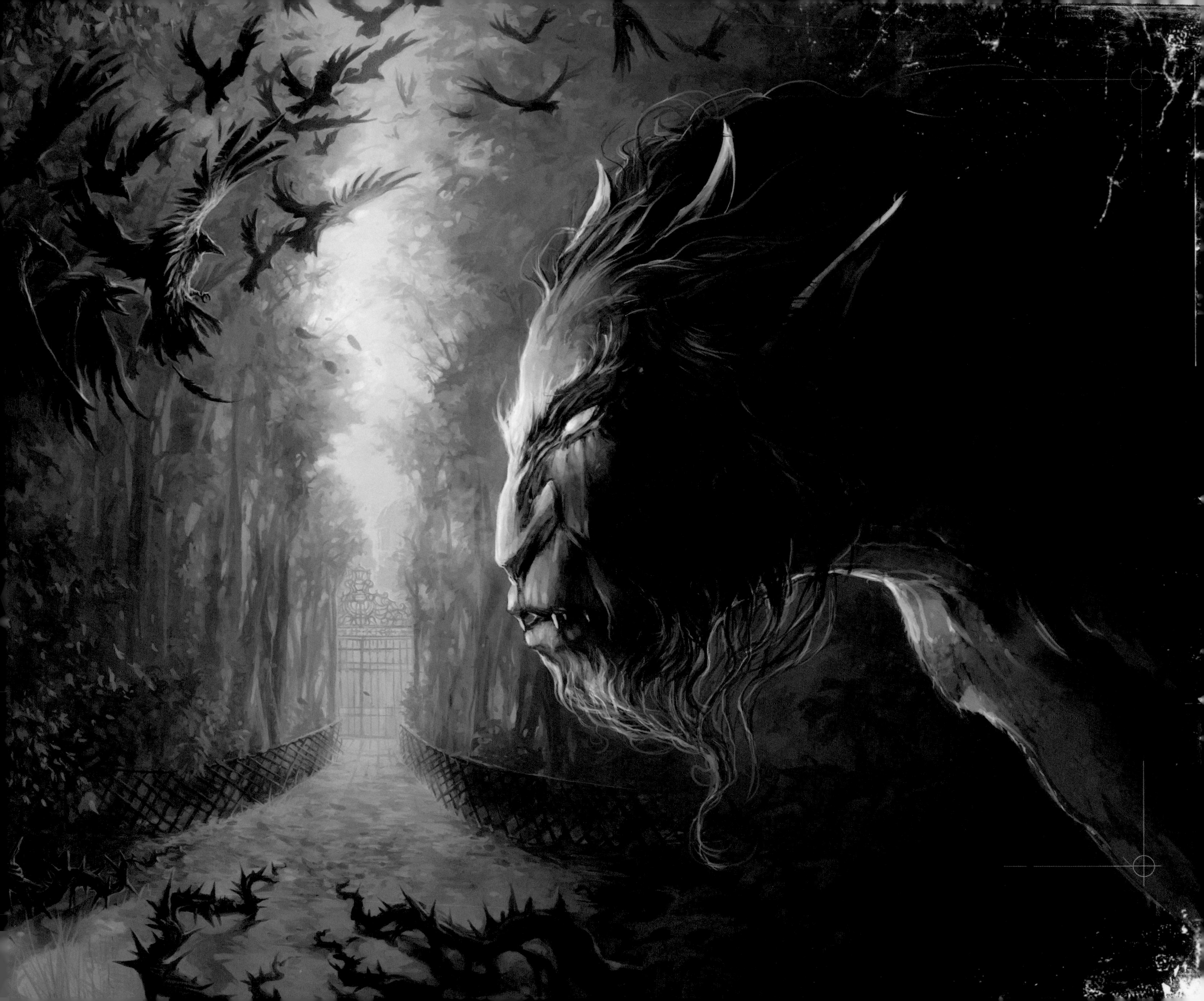

THE SHADOWS LOSE THE WAY

++++++ ++++++ While some were convinced that the gates of hell had opened in the heart of London, and others entertained lions at dinner, I stuck to my theory, at the same time laughing at the thought of *London Zoo's* exotic animals spreading out across the capital! ++++++

++++++ Comical, the giraffe in the streets of Whitechapel, but what about the Griffin flying above it? ++++++ I knew, though, not to forget the real danger here — too many long nights had gone by — *the Garden of Shadows* was no longer safe! ++++++ I needed some help, had to see things from another angle, get some distance. ++++++ ++++++

++++++ I think I should get some sleep. But there's no time. ++++++ ++++++ ++++++ ++++++ ++++++ ++++++ I must get back to work. ++++++ The Park won't be able to survive another night in the grip of this madness! And will I be able to, I wonder? My friends from the shadows will lose their way in this labyrinth. That's why *the Park of the Chimeras has a warden.* I must get to the Faun at the northern gate in order to help my friends.

++++++ ++++++ ++++++ ++++++ ++++++ ++++++ ++++++ Catching the Silvanus's eye, I immediately understood his fixation! I needed to act, and fast! This brouhaha had made me forget the most obvious thing. I needed to get the architect *Sir Decimus Burton* out of retirement. ++++++ This man who had so skillfully landscaped *the Park of the Chimeras* and its portals to the most secret of places would certainly be able to show me the right path to take.

8 - 7 - 72

++++++ This early morning incident destroyed a part of the northern enclosure of Regent's Park and at the same time made a serious breach in the fence of the ***Park of the Chimeras***! At the time of writing, there were no real casualties or irreparable damage. Unfortunately, as soon as this attack came to the attention of my friends, it awakened in them memories of the earlier hunts! The older ones feared for the souls of the young... Knowing them, they wouldn't wait for the new moon but were already closing in on the humans.

Report CII ~ B-I-b

night 02

THE HUNT FOR PHANTOMS

++++++ The hunt for phantoms and other hordes of demons that followed the explosion sparked an unprecedented interest in mythology among the many gentlemen hungry for the thrill of spiritualism and other hocus pocus. Sales of ghost-detector* cameras went through the roof! I was reduced to actually ripping the hundreds of compromising daguerreotypes — far too dangerous for us! — one by one from the hands of amateur journalists.

++++++ Even a police officer claimed to have captured the image of a Siren in the Thames. ++++++ A ghost sighting — impossible to deny. ++++++

++++++ Could I find time to garner more such reports, given that the next few nights would be so taken up with restoring order?

*Karunski Model 666 (folding)—modified for use with infrared ghost-detector plates.

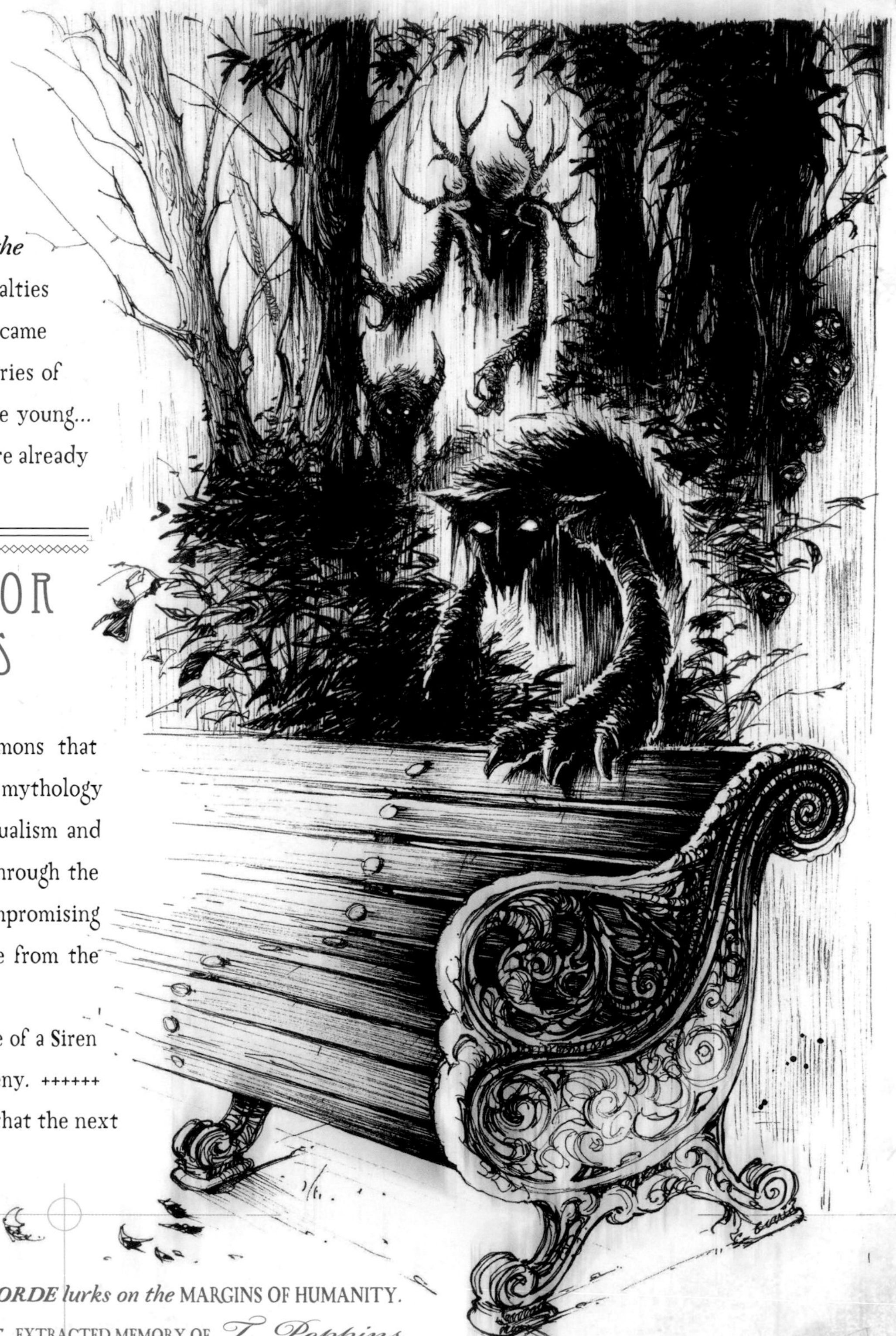

The HORDE lurks on the MARGINS OF HUMANITY.

—Regent's Park, afternoon of Oct. 10, 1874, 6:00 p.m. GMT EXTRACTED MEMORY OF *T. Poppins*

THE STAG KING

IMAGE LOCATION .... *Buckingham Palace*

ORIGINAL OWNER .... *Lord Collins*

BEASTS OF THE STEPPES

IMAGE LOCATION .... *Domain of the Wild*

ORIGINAL OWNER .... *Lady Huxleys (disappeared)*

2ᴮ

The Incident OF OCTOBER 10, 1874

Report CII ~ B-I-b

21st file

FROM THE YEAR 1874

CALL FROM THE PARK

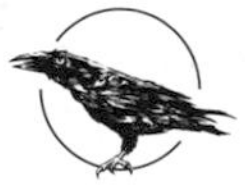

12 UMBRELLA 'POPS' WITH EXTRA NUDGE

A HOLE WAS BLOWN IN THE NORTHERN SECTION OF REGENT'S PARK THIS MORNING AT 5 A.M. - GMT

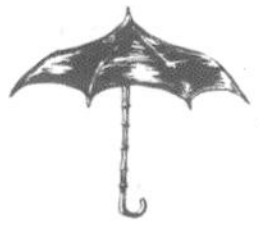

++++++ Busy days, somber nights, umbrella flights through time zones, from botanical gardens to zoological gardens... I was on my usual rounds when, on the morning of October 10, 1874, I was called back to Regent's Park. Upon my arrival, a shiver went down my spine: My worst fears had been founded. It was the silence before the storm of the explosion, and I was powerless to do anything about it.++++++ ++++++ ++++++ ++++++ ++++++ ++++++

++++++ An accident? Surely not. The deed was done. I exploded with rage! The enclosures closest to the canal had been blown to pieces, leaving the zoo animals and their keepers totally stunned. Parts of the area were in ruins.

++++++ ++++++ ++++++ ++++++ ++++++ ++++++ ++++++

++++++ The columnists were already launching into their morning headlines, not mincing their words: ***"The gates of hell open in the capital!"*** According to their articles, the explosion of a barge filled with gunpowder had unleashed legions of ghosts on Her Very Noble Majesty's subjects. ++++++

++++++ ++++++ ++++++ ++++++ ++++++ ++++++ ++++++

++++++ ***The Guild of Dream Reapers?*** ++++++

No proof, even though it bore their hallmarks...

++++++ But what of my lodgers?

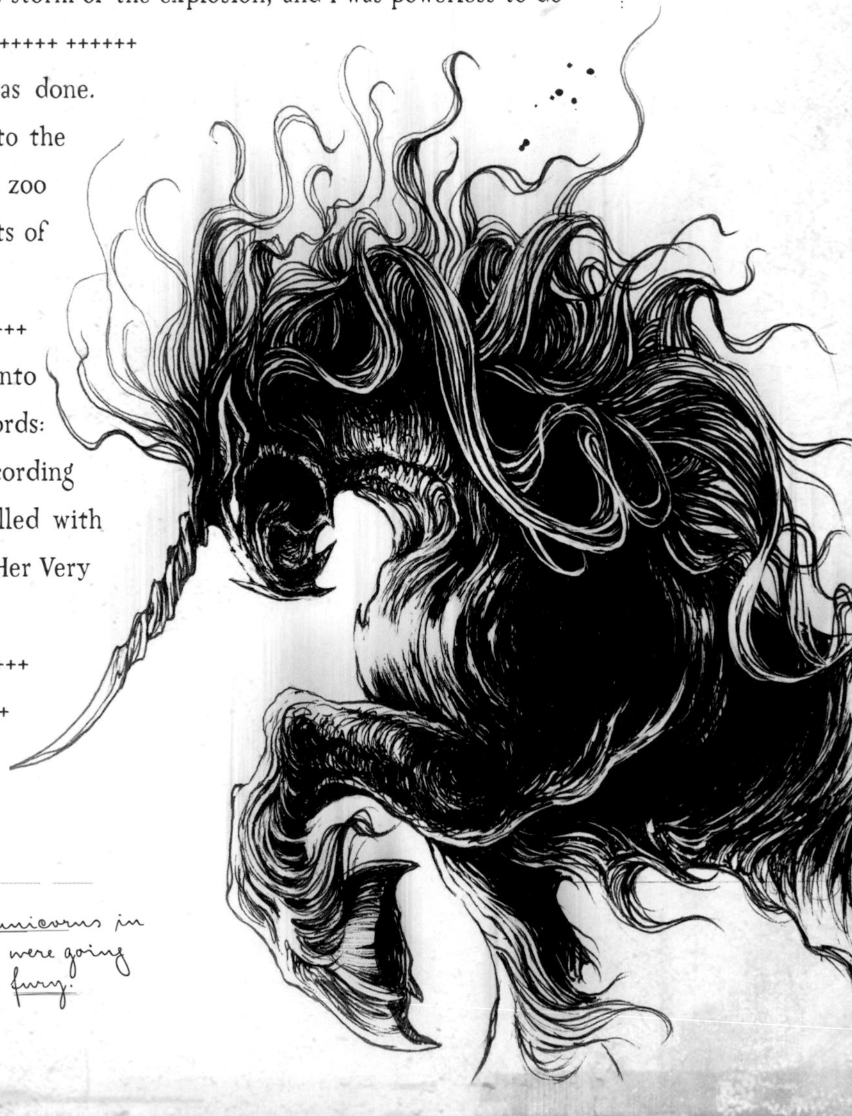

The black unicorns in the stables were going wild with fury!

2

4444444444444

THIS MORNING, OCTOBER 10TH

FEAR AND DISMAY EVERYWHERE!

LONDON ZOO SHAKEN BY A DEVASTATING EXPLOSION

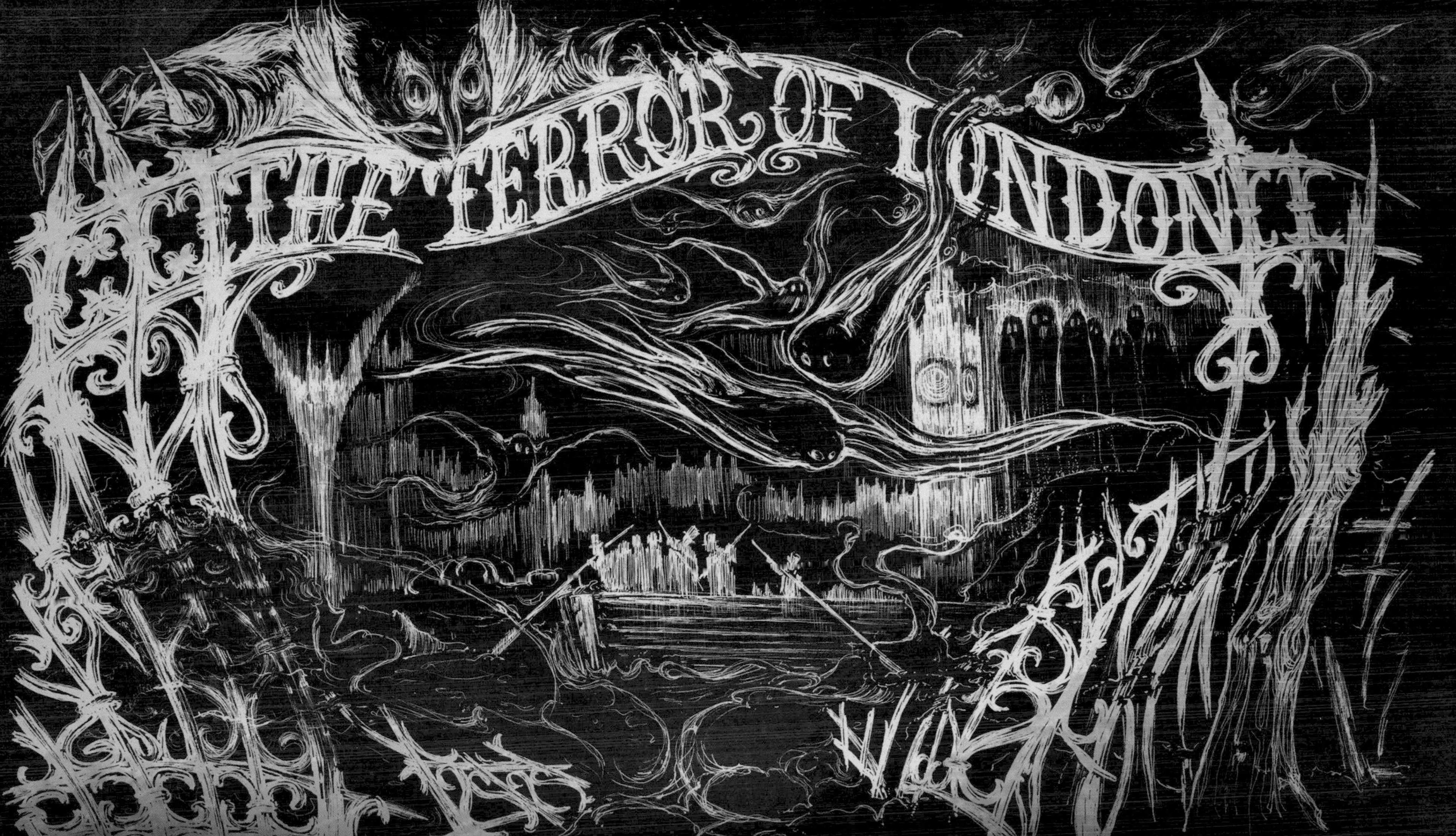
THE TERROR OF LONDON!!

HELL UNLEASHES ITS DEMONS ON THE BRITISH CAPITAL

Illustration C. Mazé

—London, October 10, 1874, 7:30 a.m.GMT - CITY ARCHIVE IMAGE VIA *Orakilum*

THE INCIDENT
OF
OCTOBER 10
1874

4

102nd REPORT {book 1-b} — *Regent's Park*

8 - 7 - 72

YEUN ELEZ, DEC. 27, 530 - 6:12 A.M. - GMT

1B

111011 111

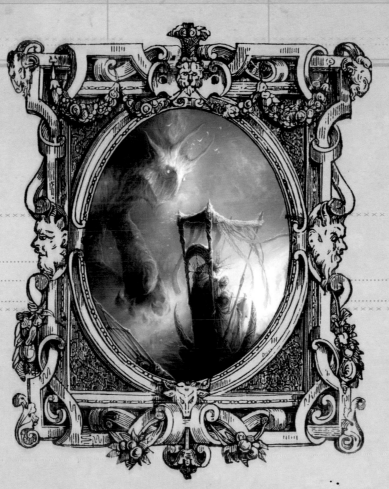

December 1 8 9 9
~ T -1:18 MIN ~

READ THESE FILES CAREFULLY BECAUSE EACH ONE OF THEM
REPRESENTS A LINK IN THE CHAIN THAT WILL ALLOW THIS MAN
TO REVEAL TO THE INHABITANTS OF LONDON'S "GARDENS OF
SHADOWS" THE PATH THAT THEY BELIEVED WAS LOST FOREVER.

—PARK OF THE CHIMERAS ++++
DECEMBER 26, 1899 – 10:42 P.M. – GMT

BY AIR MAIL

Theodore P...

*You can expect my cable as soon
as it's all over !!*

1

December 1899

T -2:18 MIN

I HAVE ALWAYS FELT THAT IT WAS THIS TREMENDOUS LOSS THAT LED THE GREAT ORDER OF ARCHITECTS TO CREATE

CHIMERIC PARKS,

SANCTUARIES FOR THE LAST CHILDREN OF PAN.

++++++ I will never forget that these shelters were designed to give peace to those who had lost hope, the hope that one day these Parks would provide ***ephemeral portals*** to the Land Beyond Dreams... ++++++ ++++++ ++++++ ++++++ ++++++ ++++++

++++++ You have entrusted me with a responsibility and I have never wavered. Believe me, even if deep down I did not think it could happen, I have never stopped welcoming all the hunted, exhausted creatures who have come seeking asylum — poor souls, some hunted for decades, stuck wandering our world forever. All too often they enter the park wearing a mask of despair, a pale and wan countenance of terror. Being no more than shadows of themselves, they have become lost between two worlds, ***Cursed*** souls with hearts tortured by fear.

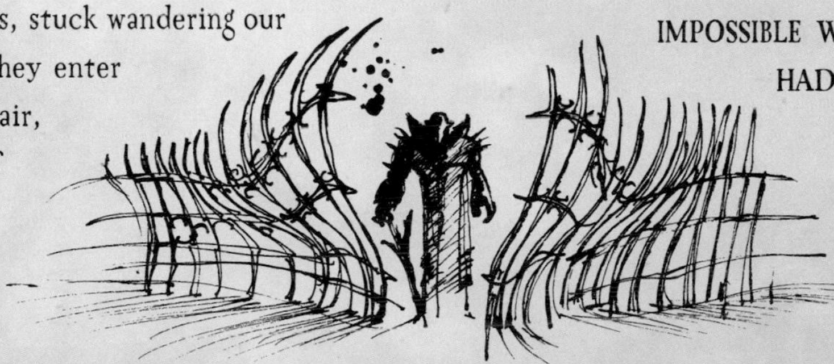

++++++ Once again you were right, because over time, this place allowed the true nature of each being to come out, little by little, and I believe I can honestly say that these places saved them.
I am convinced that these parks have become their last refuge and their last hope of one day reaching the great plains of the Land Beyond Dreams...

I KNOW FOR A FACT THAT TONIGHT, WHAT SEEMED TO ME IMPOSSIBLE WILL BECOME POSSIBLE, AND WHAT HAD BEEN SHUT WILL REOPEN.

Everything has a price, he knows that. I really hope that it will not be too heavy to bear.

++++++ ++++++ ++++++ ++++++

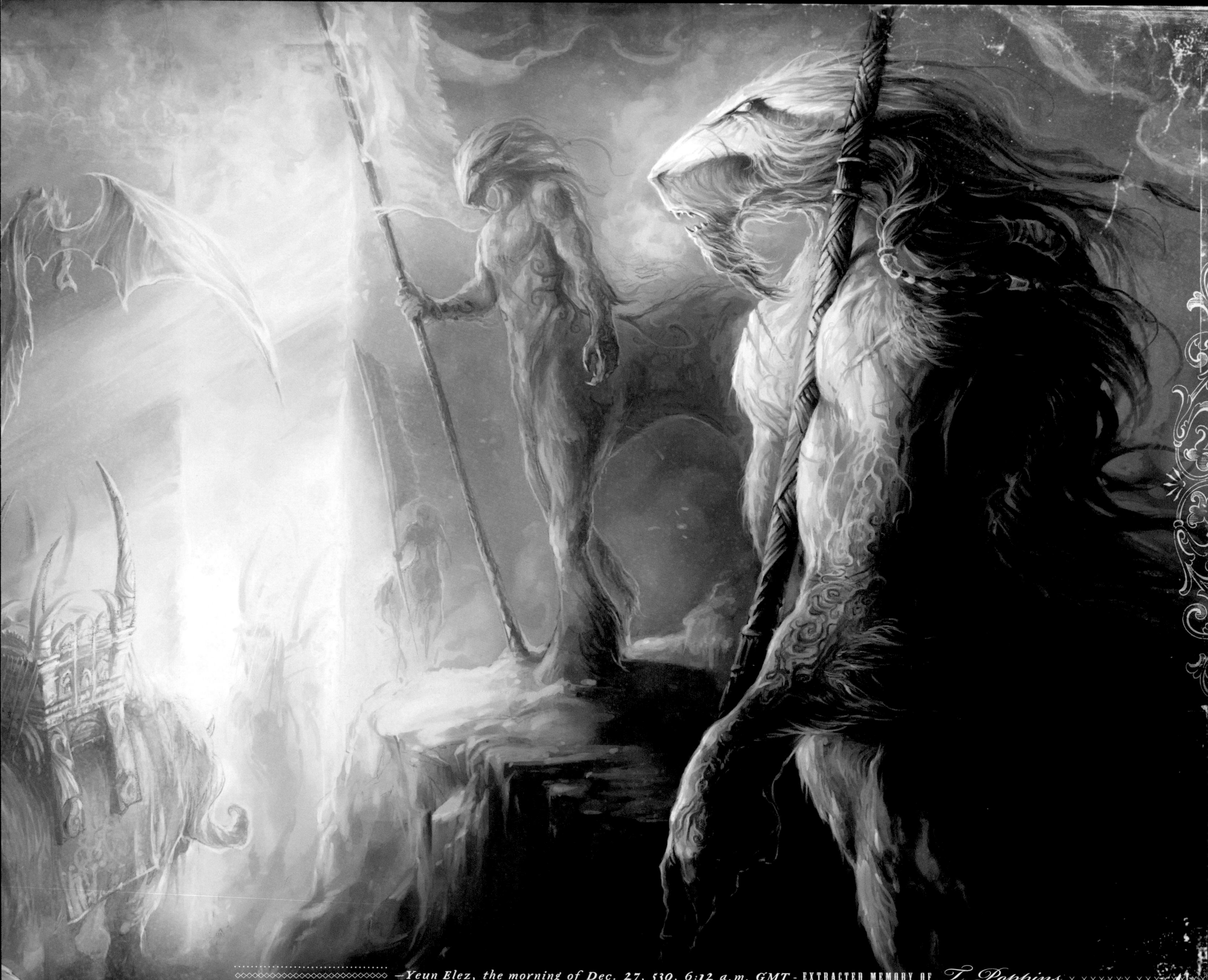

—Yeun Elez, the morning of Dec. 27, 530, 6:12 a.m. GMT - EXTRACTED MEMORY OF *T. Poppins*

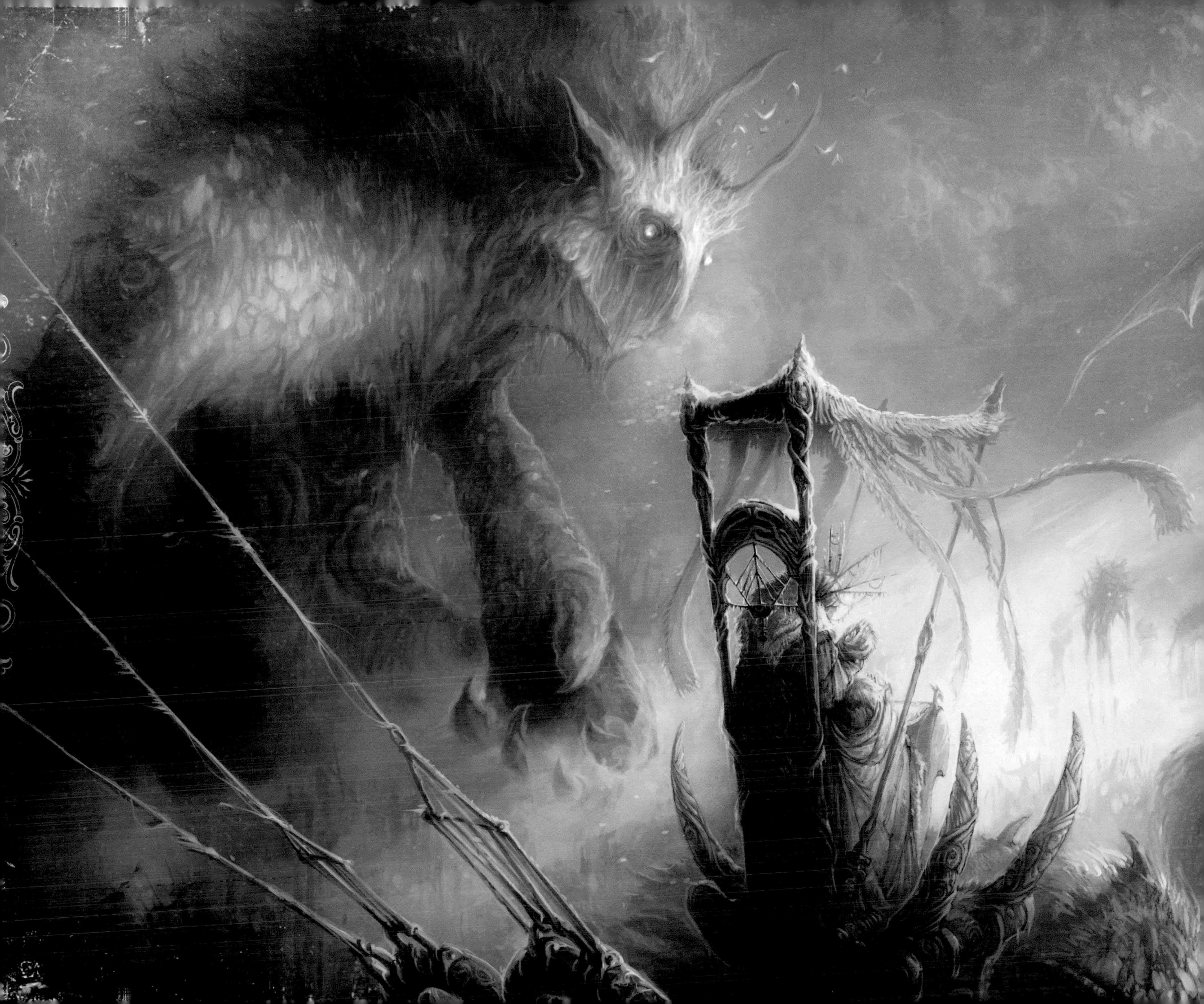

IN HUMAN MEMORY THERE HAS BEEN NO GREATER MASSACRE!

++++++ ++++++ ++++++ ++++++ ++++++ ++++++

BY PERFORMING THESE AND OTHER ACTS THAT WILL FOREVER BE ETCHED IN OUR MEMORIES, THEY HAD FINALLY LOST ALL SEMBLANCE OF BELONGING TO THEIR SO-CALLED "HUMAN" RACE!

++++++ My sadness deepens as I remember that December morning on the bloodied moors of *Yeun Elez* when we silenced the *song of swords* and opted for the *Great Exodus*.

++++++ ++++++ ++++++ ++++++ ++++++ ++++++ ++++++ ++++++ ++++++

++++++ In human memory there has been no greater massacre! That day, too many souls left the earth, too many brothers perished, obligating Pan to do what had to be done in order to ensure the safety of his beings. They had to flee the madness of Man, flee those senseless hunts and take refuge in another world. A world created uniquely for them where they would be safe forever: the *Land Beyond Dreams*.

THAT DECEMBER
MORNING

~ THE EXODUS ~

TO THE LAND
BEYOND
DREAMS BEGAN

++++++ ++++++ ++++++ ++++++ ++++++ ++++++

++++++ It is said that afterward this place was cut off from our world to keep out the *Reapers* who hunted them relentlessly. However, other writings state that Pan left some *paths* open — invisible to the eyes of Man — for those who could not follow to find their way. But unfortunately I have to admit that despite spending many long years searching for them, I have found no sign of these paths. Over time, the locations of these *Portals, Fairy Routes, Empty Pathways* and other *Hollow Hills* seem to have been lost, forever sealing the fate of the last decendants of the creatures of Pan...

... TO BE HUNTED.

++++++ ++++++ ++++++ ++++++ ++++++ ++++++ ++++++ ++++++ ++++++

++++++ *Filled with melancholy, they found themselves locked in our sad world.* ++++++ ++++++

...

3

...

It was on the back of this infamous document that they would launch the most preposterous hunt, the ***pursuit of the Shadow Creatures*** — a ruthless event where all the iniquities of human intelligence came together for purposes of innovation in the field of extermination. ++++++ ++++++ ++++++ ++++++ ++++++ ++++++ ***fantastic bestiaries***, in order to stave off boredom and to affirm social superiority over one's peers.

++++++ How many Sirens have been torn from the oceans as a result of these unfathomable acts? How many have been imprisoned in aquariums, exhibited, admired, and marveled at for their cries,

HOW MANY HAVE BEEN IMPRISONED,

EXHIBITED AND ADMIRED

++++++ A hunt whose victims' blood would sully, for all eternity, the area they called ***hunting grounds***. This enormous charade generated claims by our state's greatest families that hold to this day. It was, and still is, considered in good taste to capture and keep a ***fairy*** to play with at one's leisure, just as it was, and is, considered extremely decorous to hunt the Lycan, the Hydra, the two-headed Dragon, and all other creatures from the

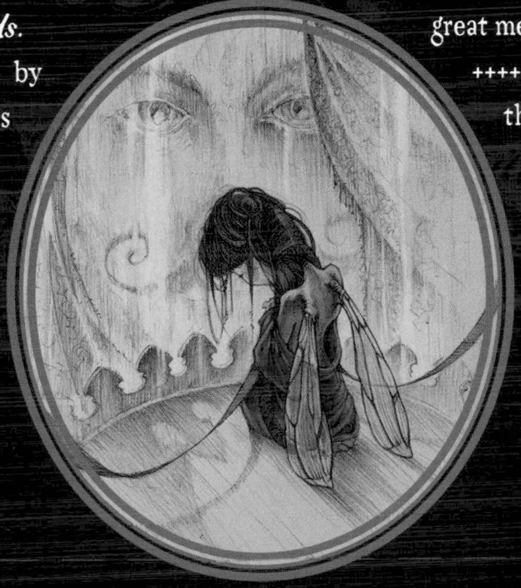

which to unsophisticated human ears are no more than a great melody.

++++++ Have they ever heard their song resonate through the height of a storm during the equinox in the great South Seas? And what about all the Titans, or more to the point, their heads, which "adorn" men's mantels as sordid trophies of prestige? Those beings disgust me; they do not deserve to be called ***men***.

...

Now that the existence of one of these first Parks is coming to an end, I can't help thinking about the events that led us to create this place, a refuge to welcome and protect the last descendants of the *Creatures of Pan*.

++++++ Know, even if we had to commit acts that some may consider inhuman, I have never regretted it. That's why, now that what has been created is about to disappear, I cannot help thinking about the reasons that are pushing me to do what must be done to protect the safe haven of the *children of Pan*.

++++++ When I recall the vile pamphlet that was brought to my attention that August 7th morning in the year of our grace 472, it awakens disgust in me for those men whose morality and values are as low as the deepest hole at the bottom of the dungeon where they drafted its contents.

++++++ ++++++ ++++++ ++++++ ++++++ ++++++

++++++ ++++++ ++++++ ++++++ ++++++ ++++++ ++++++ ++++++ ++++++ ++++++ Though not much more than the first article of this blasphemous tract remains engraved in my memory, its declaration was so despicable that my mind never completely let it go... "THE LEGITIMACY OF HUNTING, BY THE GUILD OF DREAM REAPERS: *In high society, going hunting is considered an extremely beneficial way to fight boredom. According to experienced hunters there is no better method of keeping species in balance while affirming Man's superiority over the animal kingdom and his subjects at the same time [...]."*

++++++ ++++++ ++++++ ++++++ ++++++ ++++++

...

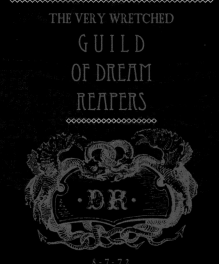

THE VERY WRETCHED

GUILD

OF DREAM

REAPERS

·DR·

8 - 7 - 72

3

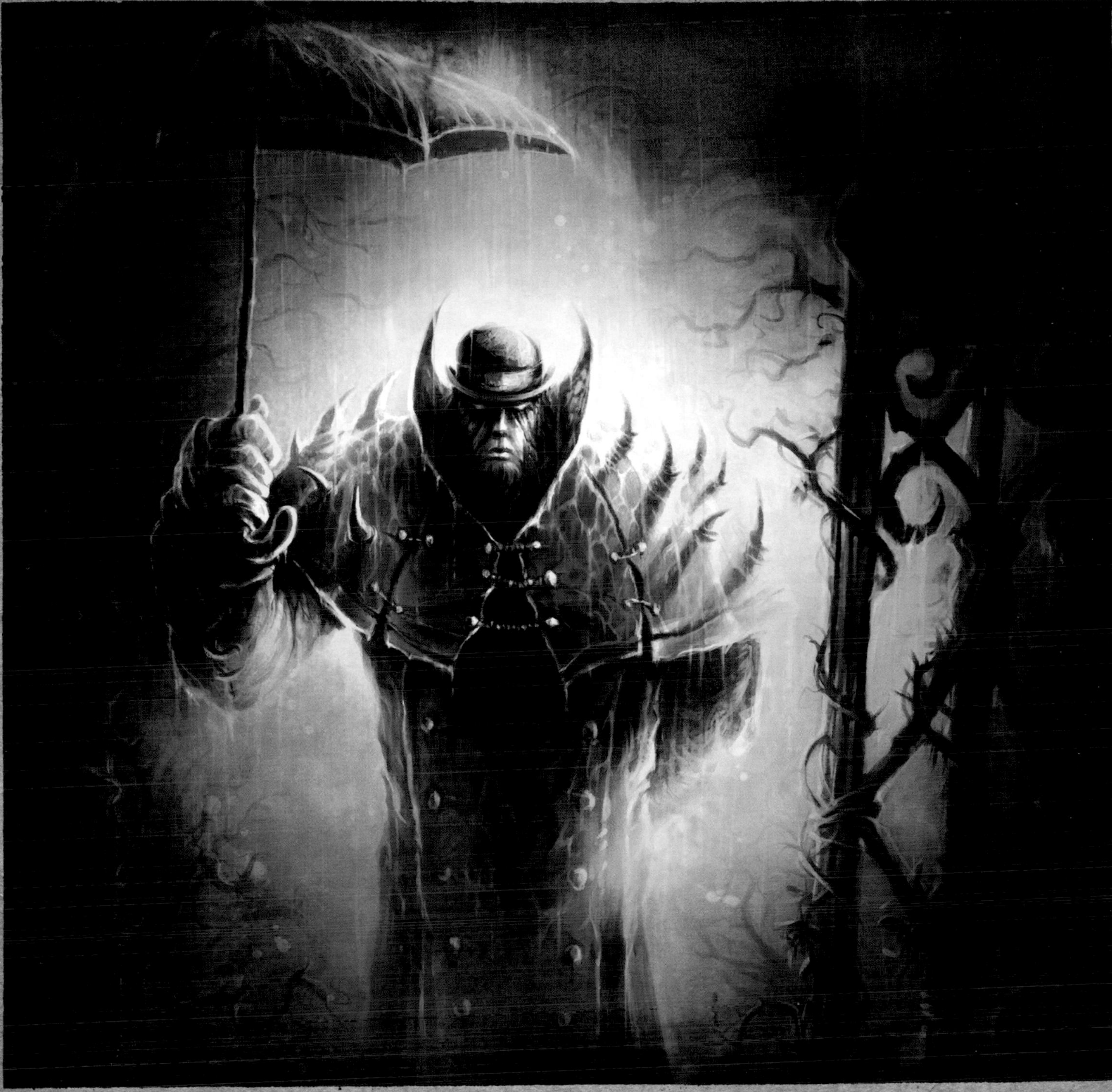

~EXTRACTION REPORT~
via ORAKILUM
MOD. 12.24

London, Chimeric Parks — CLOSING DOWN DECEMBER 27, 1899 {06:17}

– RECORDING PERIOD –
Excerpts taken from recordings made over a quarter of a century from October 10, 1874 up until
the night of December 26, 1899, without interruption.
– ANOMALIES –
The arrival of the subject, referred to as a hybrid, seems to have modified the inherent
structure of the Park of the Chimeras.

EUSTACHE LE BLANC

Sylvilagus transitionalis

ÉLIAN BLACK'MOR

Lodger - hybrid

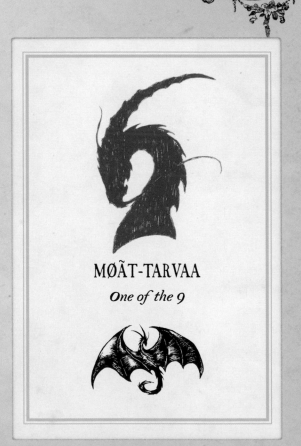

MØÃT-TARVAA

One of the 9

1

YEAR	File No.	Report No.	Place / Location	Time Period	No. of Creatures	~ Observations ~
1875	0022	0105–0108	THE 5 PARKS	××××	61	..........ADMISSION OF 5 GHOSTS + 1 FAIRY AUTOMATON + 1 BLACK SIREN..........
1876	0023	0109–0112	Kew Gardens	Autumn	67	..............ADMISSION OF A PACK OF WOLVES FROM THE STEPPES (6)..........
1877	0024	0113–0116	THE 5 PARKS	Autumn	67	....................FENCE MAINTENANCE (NTR)......................
1878	0025	0117–0120	St. James Park	Spring	! 65	..........DEATH OF THE 2 YOUNGEST WOLVES FROM THE STEPPES..........
1879	0026	0121–0124	Kensington Gardens	Autumn	66	..........ADMISSION OF KRAKEN (3 YEARS OLD)........ *make room*
1880	0027	0125–0128	××××	××××	66	..........................N.T.R....................... *+ enlarge bunks*
1881	0028	0129–0132	Hyde Park	Winter	68	..............ADMISSION ASURAS (2)............
1882	0029	0133–0136	Kensington Gardens + Hyde Park	Summer	72	..............ADMISSION DJINNS (4)............
1883	0030	0137–0140	Kensington Gardens + Hyde Park	Winter	74	..........ADMISSION 1 GORGON + 1 CENTAUR (MALE).................
1884	0031	0141–0144	Hyde Park	Summer	75	..............ADMISSION 1 MINOTAUR.................
1885	0032	0145–0148	Regent's Park	Aut./Wint	77	..........ADMISSION 1 FAUN + 1 BLACK WIDOW..........
1886	0033	0149–0152	THE 5 PARKS	March 17th	91	........ADMISSION 11 LEPRECHAUNS + 3 BROWNIES.......... *wild!*
1887 to 1893	0034 to 0040	0153 / 0154	St. James Park	Summer	130	........ADMISSION OF A TRIBE OF KORRILS PYGMIES (39 – LOWER BRITTANY)........
		0155–0158	THE 5 PARKS	××××	130	................FENCE MAINTENANCE (NTR)................
			THE 5 PARKS	Winter	130	..........MAINTENACE LIVING ROOM/SITTING ROOM..........
		0159 / 0160	Kew Gardens	Autumn	131	..............ADMISSION 1 SCARECROW............
		0161 / 0162	Hyde Park	Summer	139	..............ADMISSION OF PIXIES (5 MALE + 3 FEMALE)............
		0163–0166	Kew Gardens	Winter	140	..........ADMISSION 1 CHUPACABRA (BRASIL)..... *Transferred to Park New World?*
			×	××××	140	..........................N.T.R.......................
1894	0041	0167–0168	Kew Gardens	Autumn	141	........ADMISSION 1 LYCAN (?)................
1895	0042	0169	××××	××××	141	..........................N.T.R....................... *Break-in*
1896	0043	0170–0172	Kensington Gardens	Summer	141	......ADMISSION CHIMERA COMPANY (48 PEOPLE)..... *Decimus*
		0173–0174	Kensington Gardens	Autumn	190	..............ADMISSION OF GOLEM........
1897	0044	0175–0178	××××	××××	190	..........................N.T.R.......................
			St. James Park	Winter	192	..........ADMISSION KNIGHTS : BLACK & HEADLESS (2)...........
			××××	××××	192	..........................N.T.R.......................
1898	0045	0179 / 0180	Kew Gardens	Winter	194 !	........ENTER – THAMES JUNK + ADMISSION HYBRID & DRAGON (?)........ *The beginning of this report is in file 45*
		0181–0182	Kew Gardens	Winter	194	..............UPKEEP PALM HOUSE..............
1899	0046	0183	St. James Park	Spring	194	..........ADMISSION 2 CENTAURS (INJURED)...........
		0184	THE 5 PARKS	Summer	×××	..........xxxxxxxxxxxx........... *(how many?)*
		0185 / 0186	Hyde Park	Autumn	198 ?	*Memory of Shadows* ....ADMISSION 1 LEPORID WITH BIG EARS........... *+ Black's revival*
		0187	THE 5 PARKS	Winter	×	..............PARK CLOSED DOWN..............

200+ !

MISS MAZE, *arch. of the Garden of Shadows*

×××××× ××   ×××× ××××××

BIBLIOGRAPHY
AVAILABLE IN FRANCE

By the same authors · Jan '05 — Oct '15

Glenat Editions :

☑ Collection `:: BLACK'MOR CHRONICLES ::`

- 'IN SEARCH OF LOST DRAGONS' (FIRST Series).

- 'THE CURSED' (SECOND series).

- 'WILD WEST DRAGONS' (THIRD Series),

  Anticipated Fall 2016 in France

....

☑ Collection `:: ENCYCLOPEDIA OF GHOSTS ::`

- 'Grisly Encyclopedia of Ghosts'

- 'Terrifying Encyclopedia of Apparitions'

....

☑ Collection `:: TEA-TIME MONSTERS SHOW ::`

- 'Everything you need to know about, and how to live with, MONSTERS'

- 'SPOOKY — MONSTER INN' (VOLUME ONE).

  Anticipated Fall 2015 in France

AVAILABLE IN ENGLISH :

- 'IN SEARCH OF LOST DRAGONS' (DYNAMITE Entertainment).

COMMENTS :

Your devoted, T. Poppins

certified BIBLIOGRAPHY   responsibility of Matilde de la Tanpiere Names TEL 0209

To the one who will always be my most beautiful adventure...
Elian B.

" [...] All this seemed impossible or even unimaginable, and yet ... ": I use his words to thank this sweet dreamer, observer of so many of my adventures...
Carine-M

Thank you to the great Drugstore team, with a special thought for "Sir Benoit" and his elegant support!
Carine & Elian

4444444444444

TELEGRAM
LAST MINUTE INFORMATION

ISBN	978-1-60887-534-4
DRAWINGS	COLORS
E.B'M	E.B'M
C-M	C-M

FROM	NUMBER	NUMBER OF WORDS	DATE REGISTERED	TIME REGISTERED	TYPE OF SERVICE
LONDON	II Cycle	idem	9/22/15	19:14	NOT CENSURED

First published in the United States in 2015 by Insight Editions.
Originally published in Great France in 2011 by Glénat Editions.
Les Maudits by Elian Black'Mor & Carine-M © 2011 Glénat Editions
Translation © 2015 Insight Editions

From an original idea created by Elian Black'Mor & Carine-M
Graphic conception & execution by: Elian Black'Mor & Carine-M
Story: Elian Black'Mor & Carine-M

Illustrations : Elian Black'Mor & Carine-M
Translation: Ivanka Hahnenberger and Nicholas Simon Cooke

AUTHOR'S SITES :
www.elian-black-mor.com
www.carine-m.com

SITE OF AUTHOR'S WORKSHOP :
www.arsenic-et-bouledegomme.com

INSIGHT
EDITIONS
PO Box 3088
San Rafael, CA 94912
www.insighteditions.com

Find us on Facebook: www.facebook.com/InsightEditions
Follow us on Twitter: @insighteditions

Library of Congress Cataloging-in-Publication Data available.

ISBN: 978-1-60887-534-4

ROOTS of PEACE   REPLANTED PAPER

Insight Editions, in association with Roots of Peace, will plant two trees
for each tree used in the manufacturing of this book. Roots of Peace
is an internationally renowned humanitarian organization dedicated to
eradicating land mines worldwide and converting war-torn lands into
productive farms and wildlife habitats. Roots of Peace will plant two
million fruit and nut trees in Afghanistan and provide farmers there with
the skills and support necessary for sustainable land use.

Manufactured in China by Insight Editions

10 9 8 7 6 5 4 3 2 1

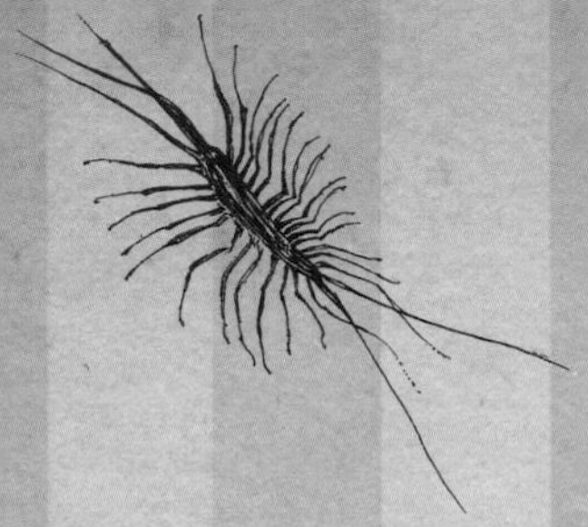

EXTRACTION REPORT ~
via ORAKILUM
MOD. 12.24

Dramatis
PERSONAE

MEMORY SYNCHRONIZATION : .... 100 % successful, prior to extraction of memories: visual & textual.

IDENTIFICATION OF SUBJECTS : ....90% successful, with exception: new subject hereinafter referred to as Elian Black'Mor.

MEMORY EXTRACTION : .... 100 % successful, for all subjects connected.

DATA RANKING : .... 100 % successful, for an independent ranking of the files.

ORAKILUM
Memory transcriber

THEODORE JOLICŒUR POPPINS
Warden of the Park of the Chimeras

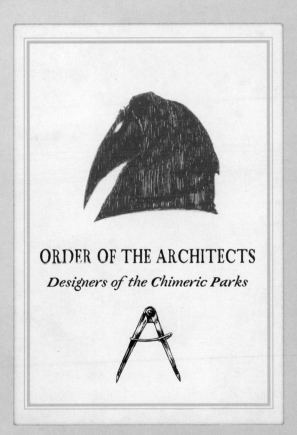

ORDER OF THE ARCHITECTS
Designers of the Chimeric Parks

~SYNCHRONIZATION MODE *Poly-holographic*~

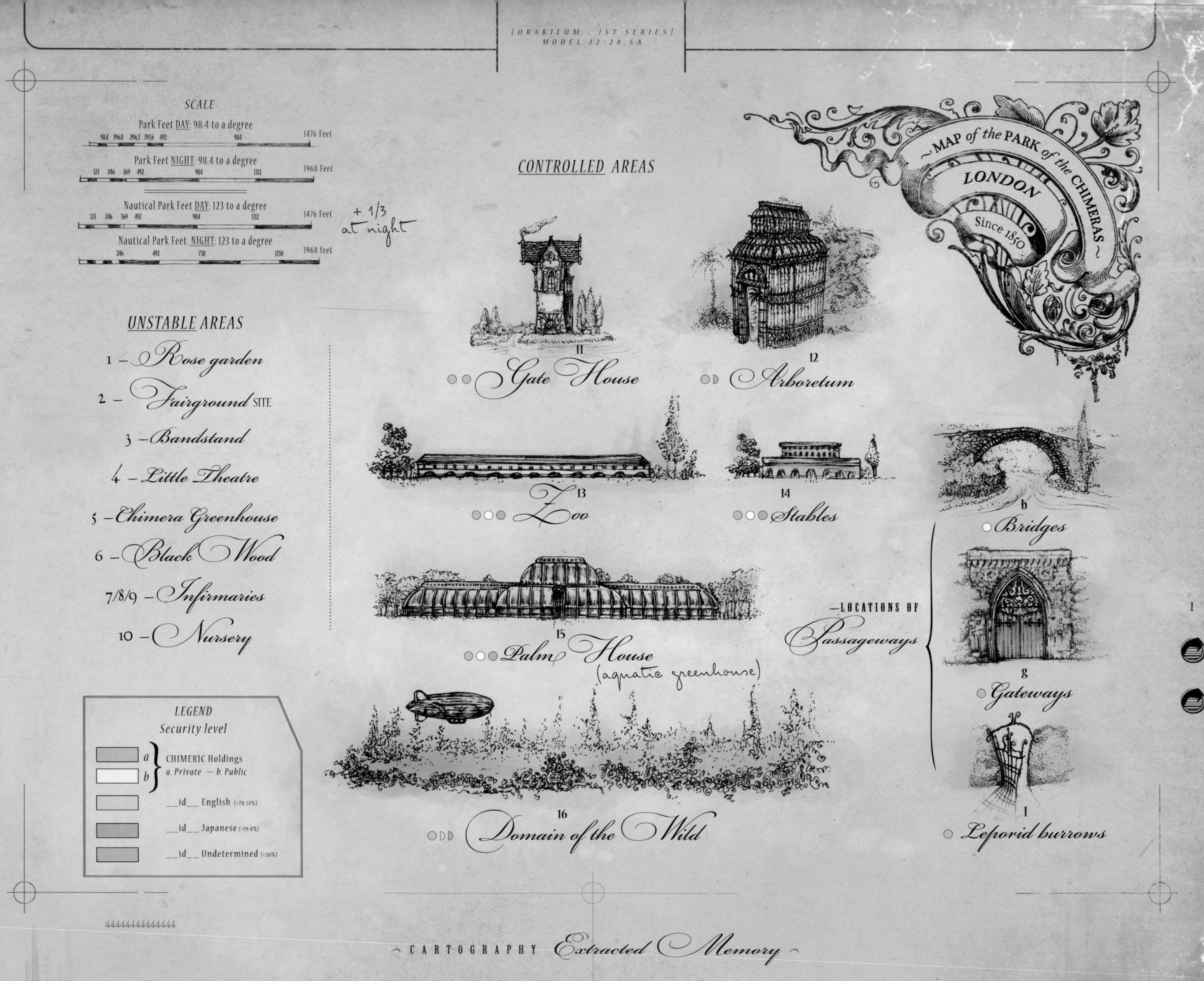
[ORAKILUM : 1ST SERIES]
MODEL 12-24.5A
SCALE
Park Feet DAY: 98.4 to a degree
98,4 196,8 296,2 393,6 492 984 1476 Feet
Park Feet NIGHT: 98.4 to a degree
123 246 369 492 984 1312 1968 Feet
Nautical Park Feet DAY: 123 to a degree
123 246 369 492 984 1312 1476 Feet
Nautical Park Feet NIGHT: 123 to a degree
246 492 738 1230 1968 feet
+ 1/3 at night
MAP of the PARK of the CHIMERAS
LONDON
Since 1850
CONTROLLED AREAS
UNSTABLE AREAS
1 – Rose garden
2 – Fairground SITE
3 – Bandstand
4 – Little Theatre
5 – Chimera Greenhouse
6 – Black Wood
7/8/9 – Infirmaries
10 – Nursery
11 Gate House
12 Arboretum
13 Zoo
14 Stables
15 Palm House
(aquatic greenhouse)
16 Domain of the Wild
—LOCATIONS OF Passageways
b Bridges
g Gateways
l Leporid burrows
LEGEND
Security level
a
b
CHIMERIC Holdings
a. Private — b. Public
__id__ English (+78.51%)
__id__ Japanese (+19.4%)
__id__ Undetermined (+26%)
44444444444444
CARTOGRAPHY Extracted Memory

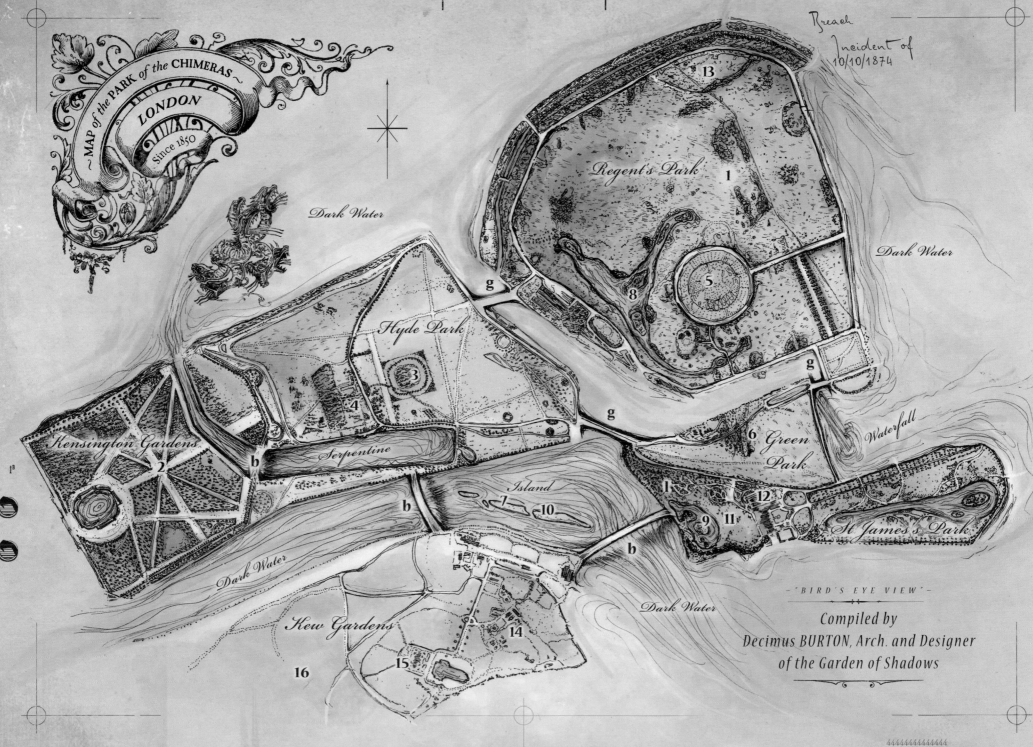

~ MAP of the PARK of the CHIMERAS ~

LONDON

Since 1850

Breach
Incident of
10/10/1874

Dark Water

Dark Water

Regent's Park
1

13

5

8

g

Hyde Park

3

4

g

g

g

6 Green Park

Waterfall

Kensington Gardens

2

Serpentine

b

b

Island

7 10

b

l

12

9 11

St James's Park

1ª

b

Dark Water

Dark Water

"BIRD'S EYE VIEW"

Kew Gardens

14

15

16

Compiled by
Decimus BURTON, Arch. and Designer
of the Garden of Shadows

~ CARTOGRAPHY *Extracted Memory* ~

FORM FOR TELETRANSCRIPTIONS VIA SYNCHRONIC POLYGRAPH

ORAKILUM

MODEL 12-24-5A-SERIES 1-SESSION 2

User .... SIR THEODORE JOLICŒUR POPPINS

Protected area .... PARK OF THE CHIMERAS:

REGENT'S PARK - KENSINGTON GARDENS - HYDE PARK -

KEW GARDENS - ST. JAMES'S PARK

Surface area .... 560 HECTARES

Population .... *over two hundred* ~~199~~

No. of polygraphs collected 1 840

Observed incidents .... 9 (SEE INDEX OF FILES)

POST-SCRIPTUM

I THINK IT IS IMPORTANT TO SPECIFY THAT THE FILES OF MEMORY
EXTRACTIONS ACCOMPANYING THE TELETRANSCRIBED NOTA BENE
NO. 238-B7 FROM THIS OCTOBER MORNING OF THE YEAR 1899 ARE
CONSIDERED THE LAST TO HAVE EVER BEEN (OR THAT EVER WILL
BE) EMITTED FROM LONDON'S PARK.

YOUR DEVOTED,

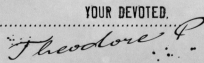

Black'Mor Chronicles

Élian Black'Mor   Carine-M

the CURSED

Welcome to the PARK of the CHIMERAS

INSIGHT EDITIONS

San Rafael, California